The Vital Role of *Pathos* in a Complete Text-Driven Interpretation of the Book of Jude

Jerry Vines

Volume 5

THE VITAL ROLE OF *PATHOS* IN A COMPLETE TEXT-DRIVEN INTERPRETATION OF THE BOOK OF JUDE

JERRY VINES

ACADEMIC THEOLOGICAL STUDIES

The Vital Role of *Pathos* in a Complete Text-Driven Interpretation of the Book of Jude
Copyright © 2025 by Jerry Vines

Published by Northeastern Baptist Press
        Post Office Box 4600
        Bennington, VT 05201

All rights reserved. No part of this book may be reproduced in any form without prior permission from Northeastern Baptist Press, except as provided for by USA copyright law.

All Scripture translations are the author's unless otherwise noted.

Cover design by Leason Stiles & Jared August

Hardcover ISBN: 978-1-953331-45-8

To Janet,
my dearest wife of almost 60 years

and to Barry McCarty, David L. Allen, and Paige Patterson,
dear friends and scholars who have aided me
in bringing this monograph to fruition.

Contents

Series Introduction	i
List of Abbreviations	iii
Preface	v
Chapter One Introduction	1
Chapter Two Pathos and Preaching	21
Chapter Three Exegetical Summary of Jude's Logos	45
Chapter Four Exegetical Summary Jude's Pathos	67
Chapter Five Using Pathos in Sermon Delivery of Preaching Paragraphs	83
Chapter Six Various Categories of Bible Interpretation as They Relate to Pathos	109

Chapter Seven
   Conclusion   125

Bibliography   137

Appendix
   Literature Review and Works Cited   153

Series Introduction

Northeastern Baptist Press publishes Christian books that inform, inspire, and encourage people to follow Jesus Christ. Realizing the need for an academic series that is tethered to the Baptist Faith and Message 2000, NEBP has developed the Academic Theological Studies (ATS) series.

The ATS series is comprised of doctoral dissertations as well as academic monographs that are carefully selected based on solid recommendations and rigorous peer review. Each study makes a unique and distinct contribution to the broader field of theology. Although all books in this series are specialized, they are not written for specialists. The ATS series provides the church at large with quality resources that have significant implications for practical issues. Toward this end, we publish within the fields of biblical studies, systematic and historical theology, Christian counseling, education, and pastoral ministry.

We foresee the ATS series growing into a significant collection of academic studies that provide the church with an accessible, yet academically rigorous avenue for theological inquiry.

Mark H. Ballard
Series Editor

List of Abbreviations

CSB   Christian Standard Bible

BDAG   A Greek-English Lexicon of the New Testament and Other Early Christian Literature

NASB   New American Standard Bible

NKJV   New King James Version

ESV   English Standard Version

SWJT   Southwestern Journal of Theology

Preface

We are currently living in an age of "feelings." Almost everywhere in our culture, the emphasis is on the emotional aspect of every situation or circumstance. F. Scott Spencer quotes Jan Plamper who says we are living during a "boom in the history of emotions; there is gold rush fever in the air."[1] He mentions also that Plamper attributes this "sharp spike in this emotional 'fever' to the cataclysmic events of 9/11."[2] Spencer continues, "To be more precise, 9/11 turbocharged a fire for understanding emotions that had been burning at the close of the twentieth century across a wide range of disciplines . . . almost every other field (in addition to neuroscience) in the humanities has caught 'emotion fever' as well, including classics, literature, linguistics, philosophy, psychology, sociology, political science, economics, and education."[3] I would add, biblical studies. The New Hermeneutic has informed much modern-day preaching to emphasize feelings. The New Hermeneutic has done so with the result that the propositional content of Scripture has often been neglected. Of course, this is one of the reasons that conservative scholars have been leery of giving much attention to ascertaining the *pathos* of Scripture.

---

    1 F. Scott Spencer, editor, *Mixed Feelings and Vexed Passions: Exploring Emotions in Biblical Literature* (Atlanta: SBL Press, 2017), 1.

    2 Spencer, *Mixed Feelings and Vexed Passions,* 1.

    3 Ibid., 1-2.

THE VITAL ROLE OF *PATHOS*
IN A COMPLETE TEXT-DRIVEN INTERPRETATION OF THE BOOK OF JUDE

Gregory K. Hollifield helpfully illustrates the value of the study of *pathos*:

> A rudimentary knowledge of the dynamics of *pathos* can serve the preacher who wishes to bring his exposition of the Scriptures to life. Recovering the mood of the text, regulating his own emotions by submitting to those of the text, and recreating those emotions within the listening audience will influence what he says, how he says it, and how it is received. The resulting difference might be compared to listening to a song in "surround-sound stereo" rather than from a static-filled transistor radio."[4]

Through 60+ years of consecutive book-by-book preaching, I have sought to give a careful, thorough interpretation of Scripture in preaching paragraphs through each Bible book. Careful attention was given to the structure of the preaching paragraph, intensive word studies, grammatical studies, and a resulting application of the preaching paragraph. The steps followed have been discussed in several volumes on preaching I have written (*Power in the Pulpit, Progress in the Pulpit,* and *Passion in the Pulpit*).

Though there was somewhat of an unconscious consideration of passage *pathos* through the years of expository preaching through Bible books, there was no conscious realization of the dynamics involved in recognizing, analyzing, and utilizing passage *pathos* in Scripture interpretation. Only in recent years have I been made aware of the concept and value of *pathos* in doing thorough Bible interpretation. I had not been aware of the available tools to assist me in delving more fully into the tone of Scripture passages. The dissertation of Adam Dooley and recent books have made these useful tools not only available to me but to all who interpret and preach the Word (see Dooley's dissertation,[5] the groundbreaking volume, *Text-driven Preaching*,[6] etc. The result

---

4 Greggory K. Hollifield, "Expository Preaching That Touches the Heart," *Preaching* 19 (2004): 18-23.

5 Adam Dooley, "Utilizing Biblical Persuasion Techniques in Preaching Without Being Manipulative," Ph.D. diss. presented to the faculty of The Southern Baptist Theological Seminary, May 2006.

6 Daniel L. Akin, David L. Allen, and Ned L. Matthews, *Text-Driven Preaching: God's Word at the Heart of Every Sermon* (Nashville: Broadman and Holman Ac-

of these new insights resulted in my most recent book on preaching, *Passion in the Pulpit,* co-authored with Dooley.

The vital role of adequate *pathos* interpretation was helpfully seen in preaching through the book of Jude. In the course of preparing the messages, I made an unexpected discovery. A survey of a number of commentaries, both exegetical and devotional, made it very clear that inattention to interpreting the emotional mood of each preaching paragraph could result in a skewed view of the overall purpose and message of the book.

Thesis

Although *pathos* has been recognized as a vital part of discourse since Aristotle included it with his other two modes of persuasion, *ethos* and *logos*, this monograph will argue that *pathos* has not been given adequate consideration in the interpretation of passages of Scripture. This will be demonstrated in the widespread failure of exegetical and devotional works to give a full analysis of Scripture *pathos* in the preparation of a series of text-driven messages from the book of Jude.

Background

In *Passion in the Pulpit,* I joined Adam Dooley in asserting the vital importance of *pathos* in giving an adequate interpretation of biblical passages. In my section of each chapter, it is indicated that what Dooley gives as an academic underpinning for proper *pathos* interpretation, I did instinctively throughout preaching series of messages through books of the Bible. Combining my instinctive analysis of biblical *pathos* with Dooley's explanations piqued my interest in the matter of adequately interpreting the emotional tone or *pathos* in biblical periscopes. This has led me to an in-depth study of the subject, including study of the meaning and expression of the emotions, historical background, and the understanding of emotional modes in Graeco-Roman and Hebrew cultures.

This naturally led to a study of emotions in the various genre of Scripture. Though not equally fruitful, every genre of Scripture has *pathos* as a part

---

ademic, 2010).

of the revelation of God's message to mankind. For instance, the various psalms are abundantly filled with all kinds of emotional expression. On the other hand, some of the didactic sections of Scripture are not as fruitful. But I take the view that the same Holy Spirit who inspired the *logos* (content) of Scripture likewise inspired the *pathos* (emotional mode) of Scripture.

So, the question arises, why use the New Testament book, Jude, as the basis for demonstrating the thesis of my monograph? The question is a good one. Obviously, Jude is not as fruitful in the study of emotional content as many other Bible books. But, in a rather intense study of Jude, I came to see that a failure to understand the envelope effect of the opening verses (vv. 1-4) and the closing verses (vv. 17-25) leads to inadequacy of interpretation and the love of the author that precedes and follows the harsh, condemnatory middle portion of this small, sometimes neglected book. To miss the emotional setting of the book is to miss the compassionate, loving, caring emotions of the author, Jude.

Methodology

The methodology of this monograph will be to recognize that each of the main passages in the book of Jude has not only a *logos* interpretation (that is, the content and intellectual meaning), but also a *pathos* interpretation (the emotional mode). The monograph will draw heavily on my previous works and will utilize insights from many others as well.

This monograph will begin with a wide view of emotion in general. Some history and consideration of the study of emotion as a general subject will be given in summary form. The focus will narrow to brief surveys of the importance and study of *pathos* in the Graeco-Roman world and Hebrew culture. After these preliminary investigations, the monograph will set forth the main tools necessary to an understanding of *pathos* in any similar body of work. These discussions will draw heavily on *Passion in the Pulpit*.

The subject matter will again become more precise. Both the Old Testament and New Testament books and paragraph sections of each book have emotional meaning as well as intellectual meaning. Both will be given consideration for the purposes of balanced interpretation, that is, *pathos* as well as *logos*.

Preface

There are certain limitations to the investigation of *pathos* in biblical interpretation. There is no attempt to give an extensive review of the general study of emotions. There is no effort to exhaustively present the Greco-Roman or Hebrew history of the study of emotions.

There could not be a complete study of the *pathos* in every book, chapter, or passage in the entire Bible. This would go far beyond the limits of this monograph. Such an effort would require many volumes of extensive *pathos* interpretation, although it is the intention of this monograph to inspire and encourage such.

The focus of the monograph will zoom in for a closer view of passage *pathos*, specifically in the New Testament book of Jude. To that end, there will be a general summary discussion of the *logos* of each preaching paragraph.

Then, the monograph will give an in-depth study of how to discern the emotional tone of each of the main paragraphs in Jude. The author will demonstrate that there is a specific *pathos* in the opening (vv. 1-4) and closing paragraphs (vv. 17-25) that constitutes an inclusion for the middle paragraphs of Jude (vv. 5-10 and vv. 11-16).

Careful attention will be given to the implementation of verbal, vocal, and visual elements in the actual preaching of the specific pericopes. These areas will give clear approaches to how those who preach and teach God's Word may convey not their own emotion, but the emotion of the preaching passage itself, so that those who hear might experience the passion of Scripture, not merely that of the preacher.

The monograph will conclude with some encouragements and suggestions for a greater sensitivity to Scripture *pathos*. The desire of the writer is that this monograph will make a positive contribution toward more consideration of *pathos* interpretation in exegetical and expository commentaries as well as devotional and sermonic works that will result in calling attention to and the implementing of *pathos* interpretation on the part of those who teach and preach Scripture. Later research led to an understanding that linguistic and socio-rhetorical works are fruitful sources of biblical *pathos* interpretation. Specific suggestions are given about how to get the fruits of such study to those who preach and teach God's Word. Such considerations should enhance the efforts of preachers and teachers as they convey Scripture's meaning and application.

THE VITAL ROLE OF *PATHOS* IN A COMPLETE TEXT-DRIVEN INTERPRETATION OF THE BOOK OF JUDE

And, ultimately, it is my desire that those who read and hear will apply these principles to biblical understanding, application, and transformation leading to Christlikeness of life.

Scope of Study

Paige Patterson shares interesting insights relative to the difference between the Greek concept of *pathos* and that of Christian preaching. He says,

> Though the Greeks would not approve, *pathos* is what made Christian preaching different than Greek rhetoric. *Logos* and *ethos* remain constant. *Pathos* goes far beyond "feeling." Feeling is not neglected, but you could have feeling divorced from *ethos* and *logos*. Such would not be *pathos*. Perhaps a better English definition might be "motive," incorporating the motive of the author or speaker as well as the motivation of the listener to action. Feeling must be there, but *pathos* commands all the resources of the human person. . . . A Greek Rhetor would acknowledge all this but be at a loss to practice it in most cases, lacking the, "thus saith the Lord."[7]

Another distinction must be made in a study of *pathos* as it relates to Christian preaching. To seek to gain the *pathos* of a given Scripture passage is really to seek the heart of God. As we shall see, God is a God of *pathos*. The interpreter must, of course, exegete the vocabulary, syntax, and central meaning of each passage. But the work is not done until he has found the heart of God in the passage.

Chapter one introduces the theme of the monograph with a general historical background of the meaning of emotion (*pathos*). Martha C. Nussbaum, probably the leading authority today on the subject of the emotions, says, "Emotions shape the landscape of our mental and social lives."[8]

---

    7 Paige Patterson, email, January 29, 2019.
    8 Martha C. Nussbaum, *Upheavals of Thought: The Intelligence of Emotions* (Cambridge: Cambridge University Press, 2001), 1.

Preface

In chapter one the introduction will give attention to the role of *pathos* in Greco-Roman culture and also Hebrew culture. The almost universal recognition and acceptance of Aristotle's threefold designation of the modes of persuasion—*ethos*, *logos* and *pathos*—will be introduced. Although there is some question about the role of *pathos* in Hebrew culture, there will also be given evidences of its importance in evaluating Hebrew Scripture.

Finally, the evidences of *pathos* in the Old and New Testaments will be discussed by means of several illustrations of its importance. Matthew A. Elliott discusses the Hebrew Scripture's integration of knowledge and emotion. He says, "Notice the link between knowledge and heart in Jeremiah 3:15: 'I will give you shepherds after my own heart, who will feed you with knowledge and understanding.'"[9]

Specifically in the New Testament, Elliott distinguishes between the use of the concept of *pathos* in Hellenistic culture and in the New Testament: "This usage is very different from how the word is used in the New Testament, where it is used for both suffering and strong evil desire."[10] The link between knowledge and emotion in the New Testament will also be investigated. Elliott again states, "It is important to emphasize the consistent presence of links between cognition and emotion that appear in the New Testament."[11]

Chapter two on *pathos* and preaching will draw heavily on *Passion in the Pulpit*. With reference to Aristotle's helpful modes mentioned above, Dooley and I say, "If persuasion is our goal, interpreting a text's meaning, identifying its mood, and internalizing its *ethos* is the best way to prepare for inspiring delivery."[12]

The monograph will discuss the danger of preachers conveying their own *pathos* instead of that of a selected Scripture pericope. Also, some attention will be given to how the preaching act must be directed toward proper persuasion and not an improper manipulation. Dooley and I say, "Those who carefully exegete and explain the content of a biblical text will seldom face charges

---

9   Matthew A. Elliott, *Faithful Feelings: Rethinking Emotion in the New Testament* (Grand Rapids: Kregel Academic and Professional, 2006), 83.

10   Elliott, *Faithful Feelings*, 134.

11   Ibid., 235.

12   Jerry Vines and Adam Dooley, *Passion in the Pulpit: How to Exegete the Emotion of Scripture* (Chicago: Moody Publishers, 2018), 2.

of manipulation in the pulpit . . . Appealing to the emotions of our audience is completely acceptable as long as our text compels us to do so."[13]

Chapter two will conclude with a survey of the necessary tools to adequately discern the emotive design of a text. Genre, vocabulary, syntax, and their relation to *pathos* are given a great deal of attention. Though there are other considerations, these three hermeneutical considerations will be examined. Of genre, Dooley and I say, "My(our) goal is not to represent a comprehensive guide for Bible interpretation, but more simply to demonstrate how a consideration of genre aids our efforts to preach with biblical *pathos*."[14]

The importance of interpreting the emotional impact of the vocabulary and syntax of a Scripture passage will be discussed in some depth. Dooley and I say, "Vocabulary and syntax alone will not always divulge the Bible's tone, but they almost always give us a sense of *pathos*'s permeating rhythm."[15] As to the importance of words and syntax of a Scripture, we also say, "The words of Scripture are like a locomotive, pulling two separate cars: *logos* (the meaning of the words) and *pathos* (the emotions conveyed by the words)."[16]

Chapter three will bring into sharper focus the book of Jude as I use it as an example of the failure to give a thorough interpretation by utilizing passage *pathos*, also. Chapter three will give some summary discussion of interpreting the *logos* of a Bible passage. Though not the central theme of the monograph, there is a recognition that passage *logos* must always precede passage *pathos*.

Reference is made to the work of Paul Ricoeur who coined the concept of the worlds behind, in, and in front of the text. Kuruvilla assists us by applying these concepts to the preaching of Scripture.[17]

The "world behind the text" refers to the historical background that shapes Bible passages. Without an understanding of this background, there can be little proper understanding of the content of a Bible passage. Dooley and I

---

13   Vines and Dooley, *Passion in the Pulpit*, 55-56.
14   Ibid., 63.
15   Ibid., 82.
16   Ibid., 86.
17   Abraham Kuruvilla, *Privilege the Text: A Theological Hermeneutic for Preaching* (Chicago: Moody, 2013), 39-54.

say, "By . . . observing textual nuances through the lens of historical circumstances, we are more likely (1) to understand the fuller meaning of our text, and (2) to react in ways that are similar to the original audience."[18] Though not in an exhaustive fashion, attention will be given to the context of the historical circumstances that prompted Jude to write, under the inspiration of the Holy Spirit, such a book filled with its rather severe content.

The "world in the text" indicates what was discussed relative to genre, vocabulary, and syntax as applied to the *logos* of the book of Jude. Although there will not be given an in-depth discussion of these matters, enough examination of Jude's genre, vocabulary, and syntax will be surveyed to show the importance of interpreting a biblical passage's *logos* to prepare one to do the additional vital interpretation of its *pathos* (emotional mode).

The "world in front of the text" means what the biblical writer of a biblical passage intends to do with what he has to say. Dooley and I make reference to the helpful insight of Abraham Keruvilla that "powerful preaching is often lost in a discourse about the root meanings of words and the singular application to the original audience of the Bible . . . stopping here ignores the fact that the biblical writers anticipated a world to come, rendering the Bible relevant for every believer in every age."[19] In the content of Jude, in a summary way, I will discuss how its author intended for his words to be used for those in the future who would read them.

Chapter four drills into the preaching paragraphs of the book of Jude and examines the *pathos* contained in each of them. The previous exegetical tools discussed will be applied to each of the paragraphs. This chapter will be a rather intensive analysis of each of Jude's preaching paragraphs, seeking to analyze and carefully examine the various emotions found in each paragraph.

Special attention will be given to the opening (vv. 1-4) and closing (vv. 17-25) paragraphs and the tender emotions found in each. The main thesis of the monograph will be demonstrated by showing that these envelope paragraphs form an inclusio in the book of Jude. Failure to take these into consideration in the interpretation of Jude leads to a failure to understand and correctly set forth the overall message of the book. As John Gilmore points out, "Jude

---

18 Vines and Dooley, *Passion in the Pulpit*, 93.
19 Ibid., 105-106.

didn't spare exposing those who crept into the church but were unable to adhere to the apostolic given (v. 4)." He continues,

> Jude was not blasting his immediate audience but those once removed. Notice the affection Jude expressed in the way he addressed his readers, "dear friends." (Three times: vv. 3, 17, 20). The final words of Jude (vv. 18-25), constitute the main point of the letter. They are upbeat and positive. It is a superficial scanning of the book of Jude that leads to the opinion that Jude was nasty.[20]

Chapter five will approach the subject of using the *pathos* found in the Jude preaching paragraphs in the actual delivery of those paragraphs. The chapter will draw heavily on *Passion in the Pulpit* and Dooley's dissertation "Utilizing Biblical Persuasion Techniques in Preaching Without Being Manipulative." From these sources, the use of verbal, vocal, and visual devices to correctly preach Jude's *pathos* will be used. This chapter will be rather detailed in its application of these three devices in the preaching moment.

These strategies used in sermon delivery will be discussed also as they relate to the preacher creating the same *pathos* in the minds and hearts of the listeners as that intended in the *pathos* of the preaching paragraphs of Jude. The goal of creating positive persuasion of the listeners to the truth of Scripture will be discussed.

Also, the chapter will review again what was mentioned earlier in the monograph—avoiding preaching the *pathos* of the preacher rather than preaching the *pathos* of the passage.

Chapter six is an addition to the original format of the monograph. In further research I came to the conclusion that there should be a separate chapter to discuss the various categories of Bible interpretation as they relate to *pathos*. Included in this chapter will be three different categories: linguistic and socio-rhetorical works, exegetical and expository commentaries, and devotional and sermonic works. The chapter ties these categories together to demonstrate the need for a logical flow from one to another.

---

20 John Gilmore, *Sick Crack or Sound Crick?: Jude's Role and Relevance in the Church—Then and Now* (unpublished work, May, 1998), 15.

Preface

Chapter seven will conclude the monograph. Evidence of the positive proving of the monograph's thesis will be demonstrated. The conclusion will encourage further scholarly research in what is considered to be a neglected area of biblical interpretation. The monograph will encourage those who write exegetical and expository commentaries as well as devotional and sermonic works to give a prominent place to a thorough hermeneutic of all biblical passages in addition to Jude's passage *pathos*. Several suggestions will be made to encourage those who preach and teach God's Word to make a consideration of *pathos* an essential part of their sermon or lesson preparation.

I will be forever grateful to my major professor, Barry McCarty, and the dean of the School of Preaching at The Southwestern Baptist Theological Seminary, David Allen, for their encouragement, wise counsel, and direction throughout the process of developing this monograph. Special joy is mine because Dr. McCarty has been a valued friend for many years. Unusual blessing is mine because Dr. Allen is one of my own sons in the ministry. The student has now become the professor! I am also grateful for the entire School of Preaching faculty. Their scholarship and seminars have been of great assistance to me.

I must express gratitude to my wife of almost 60 years. Janet has been by my side through this journey of preaching the Word of God. Her assistance in making hours of study possible for me cannot be underestimated. I am grateful for her love, her friendship, and her example of putting the *pathos* of Scripture into one's life and service.

I am thankful to our Lord Jesus Christ for saving me, calling me into the ministry, and giving me the opportunity to preach His Word. His grace has abounded toward me.

Chapter One

Introduction: Historical Background

A Brief Study of Emotions

The baby comes into the world crying. Emotion. The elementary school girl cries, "Sticks and stones may break my bones, but words will never hurt me." But they do. Emotion. The football star runs all the way for a touchdown. He celebrates. So do his teammates. So do the fans. Emotion. The doting father weeps as he brings his daughter down the wedding aisle to give her away in marriage. Emotion. The aging couple embrace and share moments of joy, nostalgia, and love at their fiftieth wedding anniversary. Emotion. The family gathers around their dying mother and tearfully bids her, farewell. Emotion.

Emotions. We all have them. Martha C. Nussbaum, perhaps the leading authority today on the subject of emotions says, "Emotions shape the landscape of our mental and social lives.[21] She continues, "Like the 'geological upheavals' a traveler might discover in a landscape where recently only a flat plane could be seen, they mark our lives as uneven, uncertain, and prone to reversal." [22]

Many fields pursue study of the emotions. Psychology, sociology, physiology, neuroscience, and a number of other fields interact with emotions as they apply to their field. Does the study of emotion have a place in Scripture interpretation and proclamation? This monograph will argue that the study of

---

21   Nussbaum, *Upheavals of Thought*, 1.
22   Ibid.

emotion as it relates to careful and complete biblical interpretation and proclamation requires an essential place. Further, the monograph will argue that understanding the emotional mood of a given Scripture passage contributes a necessary element of full and complete Bible interpretation.

Konstan compares what he calls the science of the emotions to architecture. He says that including emotional interpretation gives a complete interpretation, "just as architecture (or house-building, in Aristotle's phrase) informs us how to build a structure that will protect us from the elements . . ."[23]

Definition of the word "emotion" can be elusive. The etymology of the word does not hide from us. The word comes from a Latin verb, *movere*, meaning "to move." But, just how may emotion be defined? Does it have a valid place in the interpretation of Scripture and its proclamation? Lucy Hogan and Robert Reid are helpful in this matter. They discuss the involvement of emotion to the preaching of the gospel, giving an excellent presentation of the role of emotion in preaching and the means that may be used to include emotion by the vehicles of images and imagination.[24] Though not easy to define, a working definition of emotion should suffice in the purpose of this monograph. Emotion may be defined as a deep feeling that comes from within a person, issuing in a response to surroundings or such feeling that derives from relationships with other people.

Animals have emotions. Though some would demur, observation seems to indicate this to be the case. Gorillas get angry; cats sympathize. Deer fear danger; monkeys get happy. Writers as far back as Darwin link humans and animals in their shared emotional responses. Assuming his theory of evolution, Darwin says, "The community of certain expressions in distinct though allied species, as in the movements of the same facial muscles during laughter by man and various monkeys, is rendered somewhat more intelligible, if we believe in their descent from a common progenitor."[25] Based upon his evolutionary assumptions, he summarizes, "I have now described, to the best of my ability,

---

[23] David Konstan, *The Emotions of the Ancient Greeks: Studies in Aristotle and Classical Literature* (Toronto: University of Toronto Press, 2006), 37.

[24] Lucy Lind Hogan and Robert Reid, *Connecting with the Congregation: Rhetoric and the Art of Preaching* (Nashville: Abingdon Press, 1999), 75-77, 84-85.

[25] Charles Darwin, *The Expression of the Emotions in Man and Animals* (London: Penguin Books, 2009; first published in 1872), 77.

the chief expressive actions in man, and in some few of the lower animals."[26] Of course, his views and postulates do not convince those who hold to God's distinct creation of mankind, rather than the evolutionary model. To paraphrase often-used summations by creationists: Animals show no signs of the emotions related to the worship of God. When did we ever see a cow with tears in its eyes on its knees in heart-moving prayer? When did we ever see hippos rejoicing over the baptism of their young?

A goodly number of writers who may not be creationists also reject the idea that emotions provide the same responses from people as animals. Pre-dating Darwin, even Aristotle recognized the differences between man's emotional experiences and those of animals. W. W. Fortenbaugh says in that regard, "Aristotle withholds from animals: namely, the capacity for thinking . . . or intelligence. Humans have the capacity to think and therefore can believe that an insult has occurred and that some danger threatens. Animals lack this cognitive capacity and therefore cannot experience emotions as analyzed by Aristotle."[27]

David Konstan also challenges the Darwinian view that man and animals have basically the same emotions. He says that Darwin, in extending the idea of evolution to human beings, "touched on even more hallowed ground, for he now related the inner or emotional life of human beings to that of the more primitive species from which mankind had evolved."[28] He goes further, rejecting more modern attempts to make all emotions common to humans and animals. Arguing that the attempt to assign a limited set of emotions to both "is vulnerable also to the criticism that the information communicated by facial and other gestures is not as consistent . . ."[29]

According to Scripture, angels have emotions. Angels demonstrate the emotion of anger, as seen when "The Angel of the Lord" is angry when Balaam abuses his donkey (Num 22:32-33). Angels experience joy, as evidenced when the angels appear to the shepherds in the fields to announce the birth of Christ, "I bring you tidings of great joy . . ." (Luke 2:10). Abundant evidence affirms

---

26 Darwin, *The Expression of the Emotions*, 319.

27 W. W. Fortenbaugh, *Aristotle on Emotion* (London: Gerald Duckworth and Company, 1975), 94.

28 Konstan, *The Emotions of the Ancient Greeks*, 8.

29 Ibid..

that angels experience any number of emotions. A cursory look at references to angels in a Bible concordance make this apparent.

Satan and his demons have emotional responses. Scripture portrays Satan as having "great wrath" (Rev 12:12). Demons exhibit fear and strong desire. We see evidence of this when they display the emotion of fear as they beg the Lord Jesus Christ not to torment them "before the time" but to send them into the swine (Matt 8:29). A large number of Scripture references give evidence that demons express a wide range of emotions.

God has emotions. Reverently, this writer affirms that the God of the Bible is an emotional God. We see this vividly in numerous passages. A number of emotions are attributed to God: hate (Prov 6:16); love (John 3:16); anger (Rom 1:18); compassion (Lam 2:22-23). Such references abound in Scripture. God reveals Himself indeed as an emotional God, though we must be careful not to reduce God's emotions to the level of what human beings experience referred to by the same categories. Fallen human beings experience emotions imperfectly and often express them in sinful ways. Spencer says, "Human experience (is) beset by corrosive 'passions' and 'desires' (lusts) to be vigilantly nipped in the bud by rational argument, as the Stoics stress, but it was also blessed by virtuous 'sentiments' and 'affections' (loves) to be nurtured and acted upon . . ."[30] The God of the Bible experiences and expresses emotions in divine ways. An inerrant God experiences a wide range of emotions and expresses them in inerrant ways.

Scripture also presents the Lord Jesus Christ, God in the flesh, as exhibiting a wide variety of emotions. Just as God the Father experiences many emotions, so does God the Son. Because the Lord Jesus Christ reveals Himself as "the express image of His (God's) person . . ." (Heb 1:3), we expect this to be so. Jesus gets angry when He sees the hardness of the Pharisees' hearts (Mark 3:5); He feels compassion for hurting people (Mark 6:34). The Savior feels great sorrow in the Garden of Gethsemane (Matt 26:37-38); on the cross He feels not only the physical pain of crucifixion, He feels the pain of loneliness and separation from God (Matt 27:46).

---

30 Spencer, *Mixed Feelings and Vexed Passions*, 20.

Introduction: Historical Background

God the Holy Spirit has emotion. Scripture tells us of the person, work, and emotions of the Holy Spirit. From Scripture we learn that the third person of the trinity may be grieved (Eph 4:30); He also loves (Rom 15:30).

There are two primary theories relative to emotion. Emotions are cognitive or noncognitive. As to the latter (noncognitive), this view says that emotions issue in bodily responses to outside stimulating circumstances without any mental activity. The bodily reaction causes the mental reaction, so this theory goes. As to the former (cognitive), the view holds that mental activity (cognition) provides a prerequisite to emotions. Spencer concurs with Richard Lazarus who takes the view that cognition "is both a necessary and sufficient condition of emotion."[31] Lazarus says, "Many psychologists now agree that there is a large component of thought and meaning in all our emotional reactions that we construct. Far from being irrational, the emotions have a logic of their own, which is based on the meanings we construct out of the situations of our lives."[32]

The predominance of modern research into the theories of emotion takes the cognitive view. Much of this results from a "path-breaking study of Aristotle's theories . . ." Aristotle took a cognitive view on the matter of emotions. Konstan's volume provides substantial help in this regard and summarizes well the more recent tendency toward the cognitive theory of emotions.[33] Further, cognition and emotion must not be separated from one another. Spencer indicates that thinking and feeling do not stand in separation to one another, but, rather, stand interwoven with one another. He states, "Emotion, however delineated, matters a lot in human experience and can never be excised from sense or meaning making . . ."[34]

This understanding of emotion provides much help for the Christian faith and in biblical preaching also. A proper understanding of human emotions aids the presentation of the saving gospel leading to a personal experience with the Lord Jesus Christ. Therefore, the study of emotions cannot be confined to the fields of psychology, physiology, neurology, or any other secular discipline.

---

31 Spencer, *Mixed Feelings and Vexed Passions*, 20.

32 Richard S. and Bernice N. Lazarus, *Passion and Reason: Making Sense of Our Emotions* (Oxford: Oxford University Press, 1994), 6.

33 Konstan, *The Emotions of the Ancient Greeks*, 20.

34 Spencer, *Mixed Feelings and Vexed Passions*, 27.

There must be no divorce between a study of the emotions and a proper exegesis and proclamation of Scripture.

The declaration of Christian truth with correct interpretation of its emotional ramifications in addition to its propositional content is intended to result in a living out of that truth in one's actions. Elliott says, "When Christian emotions are not present, or when harmful emotions are pervasive, it is a warning that the belief system which the New Testament presents has not been grasped and valued. When Christians transfer allegiance from this world to the kingdom of God, their emotions will be transformed."[35]

Today's turn to emotions in a secular culture offers a unique opportunity for biblically correct interpretation. We currently are witnessing a turn away from language and its meaning to a tendency toward emotions, their sensations and effect. This monograph does not argue that adequate interpretation of the Bible's emotional message offers the sole necessity of interpretation for the current cultural climate. Rather, this monograph argues that while other fields of study are informative to the Bible preacher and suggest careful, scholarly research, the biblical exegete must have some foundational understanding of emotion in general to move forward in biblical exegesis and applied Christian ethics.

This monograph does argue that the biblical preacher must not run from emotion but must deal with it in biblical exposition in order to achieve a full and complete exegesis and then proclamation of biblical truth. Hershael York says, "He (the preacher) must also seek to communicate the truth that he has discerned in the biblical text in such a way that it accurately conveys the meaning—both the lexical and emotional content."[36] There is a welcome trending toward the inclusion of *pathos* interpretation that provides encouragement to this writer.

Pathos in Greek and Roman Culture

The Greeks gave emotion a name. They called it παθε or *pathos*. The student of the history of rhetoric soon finds references to *pathos*. Greece has long been

---

35 Elliott, *Faithful Feelings*, 268.
36 Akin, Allen, and Mathews, *Text-Driven Preaching*, 242.

considered the birthplace of rhetoric and thus *pathos*. As early as the speeches of the Iliad, evidence of *pathos* may be seen. The speeches of the three ambassadors to Achilles, Odysseus, Phoenix, and Ajax, seeking to persuade him to return to battle, illustrate the appeal to the emotions as a key factor in persuasion. George A. Kennedy says, "Such an appeal could be described by the rhetorical term *pathos*."[37]

Leading up to Aristotle, traces of philosophical engagement with matters of *pathos* may be traced from Socrates and Plato. Fortenbaugh says, "During the period of Aristotle's residence in Plato's Academy an investigation of emotion was undertaken which was to have profound effects upon the subsequent psychology, rhetoric, poetics and political and ethical theory."[38] To summarize Fortenbaugh's assessment, he indicates that Socrates' dialogues don't seem to give any clearly defined or elaborate theories of *pathos*.[39]

Plato seems to suggest a connection between rational thought and *pathos* but does not establish a clear relationship between them. Fortenbaugh imagines "lively debate within the Academy concerning the way in which cognition is involved in emotional response. Aristotle was most certainly part of this debate . . ."[40] While others before him seem to take the noncognitive view, Aristotle takes the cognitive view of emotion. For him, "emotional appeal would no longer be viewed as an extra-rational response and made clear that an emotion can be altered by argument because beliefs can be altered in this way, it was possible to adopt a positive attitude towards emotional appeal."[41]

In general, Hellenistic philosophers commented on *pathos* as it impacted the lives of everyday people. They were concerned with how varieties of the emotions people experienced either created negative or positive living. Having wrong emotions contributes to damaged lives. Having the right emotions results in happy, contented lives. Elliott says, "The Hellenistic schools

---

37 George A. Kennedy, *Classical Rhetoric and Its Christian and Secular Tradition from Ancient to Modern Times,* second ed., rev., and enl. (Chapel Hill: The University of North Carolina Press, 1999), 9.

38 Fortenbaugh, *Aristotle on Emotion,* 9. For the student who desires to delve deeper into the history of *pathos*, Kennedy and Fortenbaugh provide excellent sources.

39 Fortenbaugh, *Aristotle on Emotion,* 10-11.

40 Ibid., 11.

41 Ibid., 18.

compare destructive emotions to diseases of the soul."[42] Elliott gives an excellent summation of the various schools of philosophy and their approaches to *pathos*. As to the Epicureans, he says they primarily concern themselves with practical outcomes that eased "human misery and suffering." As to the Stoics, they teach that all of human emotions must be destroyed totally. The Hellenistic philosophers seek to address the wide range of emotions people of their time experience. Elliott says, "In formulating this ideal of the undisturbed life, they were responding to a society where they observed that people's emotions were often out of control. People lived with irrational fear of the gods . . . Emperors ruled according to their own selfishness . . . that led them to rule in ways that were destructive."[43]

Aristotle

Which brings us to the impact of Aristotle. His well-known and almost universally accepted three categories of persuasion enter the picture. In his "Art of Rhetoric," he delineates them as *logos*, the content of one's persuasive attempt; *ethos*, the character and the credibility of the persuader; and *pathos*, the emotional mode of the attempt at persuasion. Further, in the second book of his "Rhetoric," Aristotle deals with *pathos* in a more extensive manner. Specifically, he says, "The emotions (pathe) are those things through which, by undergoing change, people come to differ in their judgments and which are accompanied by pain and pleasure, for example, anger, pity, fear, and other such things and their opposites."[44] Paige Patterson says, "These three canons of rhetoric, though born in a pagan context, are both adequate and remarkably serviceable."[45]

Sung Gyu Kim has an interesting and pertinent observation relative to where *pathos* fits into Aristotle's means of persuasion. He says, "Aristotle believed that emotion could be changed through a logical argument. In this aspect,

---

42 Fortenbaugh, *Aristotle on Emotion*, 71.

43 Ibid., 70-78. Elliott helpfully surveys the way the Hellenistic philosophers approached the study of human emotions.

44 Aristotle, *On Rhetoric*, translated by George A. Kennedy (New York: Oxford University Press, 2007), 1.1.1.

45 Akin, Allen, and Mathews, *Text-Driven Preaching*, 17.

Introduction: Historical Background

pathos comes after *logos*. When correctly guided by reason, emotion becomes a valid and necessary motivation for action."[46]

The student of *pathos* must be cautious in correlating the Greek's meaning in general and Aristotle's more specific meaning and understanding of emotions or *pathos*. Aristotle confines his categories of *pathos* to pain and pleasure in the emotional responses of an audience. Spencer says that we must not restrict our understanding of *pathos* to these negative and positive categories. Aristotle's categories are not "absolute identification; rather (they are) . . . 'sensations' that may or may not accompany any particular emotion."[47]

The Greeks' emotions and modern emotions have similarities. Certain emotions between them certainly indicate that similarity. But this does not suggest that the emotions of the Greeks and those people experience today display themselves as one and the same. Konstan says, "The Greek emotions are specific to Greek society and to societies similar to that of the Greeks. But cultures have blind spots: we can doubtless perceive better than Aristotle himself the ways in which the pathe he describes form a coherent group. In turn, attention to classical Greek ideas of the emotions may illuminate some unclear aspects of our own emotional concepts." He gives a helpful illustration: "The cross-cultural constants in emotions are like the four elementary tastes of bitter, sweet, sour, and salty. If we rely on taste buds alone, shutting our eyes and holding our nose, then apples and onions, which have similar textures, are indistinguishable . . . Add smell, and the difference between the two is evident."[48]

Pathos becomes more structured and systematized in Roman culture. The Roman period's contribution to the study of *pathos* by its canonization of rhetoric should be considered strategic. In its historical development, the Roman Empire begins as a rather insignificant series of small city-states. Elected officials supersede the various kings who rule the city-states. The primary method for guiding the people teases out through public addresses and debate. Thus persuasive speech reigns as the optimum form of persuasion.

---

[46] Sung Gyu Kim, "The Right Use of Biblical *Pathos* in Persuasive Preaching," diss., Biola University, ProQuest Dissertations Publishing, 2013.3563286, 101.

[47] Spencer, *Mixed Feelings and Vexed Passions,* 7.

[48] Konstan, *The Emotions of the Ancient Greeks,* 261. Further study in the similarities and dissimilarities between Greek concepts of *pathos* and ours may be pursued in Konstan's volume.

Marcus Tullius Cicero

In the Roman cultural model, Marcus Tullius Cicero, commonly known as Rome's greatest orator, arrives on the scene. Cicero contributes a number of works which acquainted Roman speech givers with the Greek approach to rhetoric. Cicero's work "On Invention" is probably the major authority in Roman speech making and governing. This work becomes the "go to" authority in terms of rhetorical persuasion. In this work Cicero's famous five canons of rhetoric appear. The canons consist of (1) invention—reasoning out an argument to make it probable; (2) arrangement—organizing the structure of an effective argument in order to present the argument in the most effective manner; (3) style—presenting the speech in the most fitting words to be found so as to stir the emotions; (4) memory—with a firm grasp of the subject in order to learn how to speak without having to read the speech; (5) delivery—persuasive presentation of the argument's subject and words by means of vocal and visual means.[49]

Cicero doesn't seem to place a strong emphasis on *pathos*. Although in his "On Oratory," he affirms Aristotle's three means of persuasion "by arguing that success in oratory arises from 'the proof of our allegations, the winning of our hearer's favour, and the rousing of their feelings' to whatever the case may require."[50] Hogan and Reid also affirm that to Cicero the best orator is one who has the ability to move, teach, and please an audience."[51] Sung Gyu Kim affirms that Cicero's comments about style closely relate to general observations about *pathos*. In commenting on Cicero, Kim says, "Style is closely related to *pathos* in that style is used for persuasion through emotional appeal. Also, it is connected to both *ethos*, in that an orator's style establishes one's authority and credibility, and *logos*, in that schemes of repetition in style serve to produce coherence and clarity."[52] Further, Gyu says about Cicero's emphasis relative to

---

49 Kennedy, *Classical Rhetoric*, 98-136. The author of this monograph intends here to only give a summary of the excellent work of George A. Kennedy in chapter five, "Rhetoric in the Roman Period."

50 Hogan and Reid, *Connecting with the Congregation*, 30.

51 Ibid.

52 Kim, "The Right Use of Biblical *Pathos*," 106.

pathos that he "reckoned that winning the hearer's favor is greatly influenced by whether or not the audience's emotions are evoked."[53]

Cicero takes another step by stressing those who speak must feel the emotions first if they intend to create the same emotions in the minds of their hearers.

> Moreover it is impossible for the listener to feel indignation, hatred or ill-will, to be terrified of anything, or reduced to tears of compassion, unless all those emotions, which the advocate would inspire in the arbitrator (audience), are visibly stamped or rather branded on the advocate himself... I give you my word that I never tried, by means of a speech, to arouse either indignation or compassion, either ill-will or hatred, in the minds of a tribunal, without being really stirred myself...[54]

Marcus Fabius Quintilian

Marcus Fabius Quintilian provides the best example of extensive writing in the field of rhetoric during the Roman period. His twelve volumes on "Education of the Orator" serve as a standard for speakers during that period. Cicero's influence is evident. From Cicero, Quintilian draws his fundamentals of rhetoric, though he clearly takes the subject further and goes into more detail. Kennedy says that this work presents a setting forth of "the standard theory of invention, arrangement, style, memory and delivery."[55] Hogan and Reid say Quintilian takes the position that oratory is "the good man speaking well."[56] Quintilian establishes a broader definition than that of Aristotle's which he felt was not as broad as needed. Hogan and Reid say, "Quintilian championed the idea that learning how to 'speak well' required as much attention to the persuasive force of style and arrangement as knowing how to make plausible arguments."[57]

---

53 Kim, "The Right Use of Biblical *Pathos*," 108.
54 Cicero, "De Oratore Books I, II," translated by E. W. Sutton and H. Rackman, *The Loeb Classical Library* (Cambridge, MA: Harvard University Press, 1948), 2.189).
55 Kennedy, *Classical Rhetoric,* 115.
56 Hogan and Reid, *Connecting with the Congregation,* 30.
57 Ibid., 31.

Quintilian also placed emphasis on the orator feeling "the same emotion that they want to arouse in the judge. In addition to identification, in order to make emotional appeal, Quintilian strongly recommended that orators be very good at vivid descriptions through word pictures and the uses of imagination and metaphor."[58] This area of the use of *pathos* will be discussed in later chapters.

Publius Cornelius Tacitus

Admiration for the oratorical skills of Roman historian Publius Cornelius Tacitus led those of his time to value his insights into oratory. His *The Dialogue on Orators* had wide readership during his time. In this possible or imaginary meeting of Roman orators, one of them laments the corruption of the times and submits that there is a widespread "decline of eloquence." Another orator praises "the eloquence of the past and criticizes that of the present as more the art of an actor than an orator."[59]

In summary, the overall understanding of emotion in terms of its definitions and examples in a variety of settings is informative for the purposes of this monograph. Also, the historical context of both the Greek and Roman emphases on the use of *pathos* in persuasion give us additional insights for purposes of biblical interpretation and sermonic proclamation of passage *pathos*. However, such areas of inquiry do not exhaust the primary primary goal of this monograph. This monograph will argue that the human biblical authors did not rely on human sources for their compositions. Rather the argument will be that the same Holy Spirit who unerringly inspired the human authors to give the *logos* of the passage also inspired the *pathos* found within their writings. Kim says, "It is appropriate that the 'human personal feeling' was utilized as an expression of the truth by the biblical authors under the superintendence of the Holy Spirit. In this aspect, there is no doubt that biblical *pathos* was inspired by the Holy Spirit as well."[60] Kim continues, "For this reason, it is very important to find the

---

58 Kim, "The Right Use of Biblical *Pathos*," 118.
59 Kennedy, *Classical Rhetoric,* 118.
60 Kim, "The Right Use of Biblical *Pathos*," 62.

biblical *pathos* that the biblical authors intended to deliver and to study its roles, that is, making the author's intended idea more clear."[61]

PATHOS IN HEBREW CULTURE

The primary source for the use of *pathos* in Hebrew culture, of course, is the Old Testament. This will be the focus of the next section of this chapter. Elliott's summary of Hebrew *pathos* is found in his third chapter, "Emotion in Jewish Culture and Writings." He raises several questions pertinent to a survey of *pathos* in Hebrew culture. One, do we not see the mixing of Old Testament and Greek ideas during the Second Temple period that are informative for a study of *pathos* in Hebrew culture? Also, what kinds of emotion in Hebrew culture do we find reflected in the Old Testament?[62]

Too often the view taken indicates that Hebrew culture was bereft of rhetorical training and thus no study of *pathos*. Witherington demonstrates that (there was) the inclusion of rhetoric "as a staple of early Jewish education for literate males."[63] He quotes J. Daryl Charles: "If Josephus the historian, Theodorus the rhetorician, Meleager the poet, and Philodemus the philosopher hailed from Galilee, perhaps it is indeed time to dispel the myth of Galilean illiteracy."[64] Witherington also theorizes that Hebrew workmen in the Hellenistic period, building such cities as Sepphoris, needed salesmen skills that would require rhetorical and thus *pathos* tools of persuasion.

Hebrew culture gave great emphasis to emotions as they were manifested by the righteous and the wicked. The next section of the chapter will give specific examples in the Old Testament itself. For now, a general comparison between the emotions of the righteous and the wicked will serve as an example of *pathos* in Hebrew culture. Elliott says, "One way to differentiate the righ-

---

61 Kim, "The Right Use of Biblical *Pathos*," 63.

62 Elliott, *Faithful Feelings*, 84.

63 Ben Witherington, III, *Letters and Homilies for Jewish Christians: A Socio-Rhetorical Commentary on Hebrews, James and Jude* (Downers Grove: InterVarsity Press, 2007), 564.

64 Witherington, *Letters and Homilies for Jewish Christians*, 564.

teous from the wicked in the Old Testament is by how they feel."65 The words used to describe each seem to be the words that were current in the Hebrew culture of the time. Writing about David's failings, Childs shows that David, a man after God's own heart, illustrates a godly person's emotions, even in times of great sin. Childs says, "His character shows us what godly emotions are to look like."66

The vocabulary of the Hebrews illustrates the place of *pathos* in their culture. Perhaps two examples will illustrate the point. When the Hebrews referred to knowledge, the verb used to convey "'to know' possesses a rich semantic range within which the senses predominate. Emotional ties, empathy, intimacy, sexual experiences, mutuality, and responsibility are all encompassed within the usage of the verbal stem."67

The Hebrew word for "to know" is often linked in Hebrew culture to a word for the heart. Elliott says that the linkage of these words provides "an integration of knowledge and emotion. Thus, to the Hebrews, knowledge as they use it is heartfelt and emotional."68

The words used in Hebrew culture for the emotions of the wicked provide insight into the meaning of *pathos* as expressed by them. The words for what the wicked love and hate open the door to the Hebrews' understanding of emotional expression. One example aptly illustrates this. Elliott says, "The wicked love evil and desire to do wrong. Their basic emotional disposition is fundamentally opposite from the righteous . . . For the wicked, it is a lack of knowledge or no desire to obtain right knowledge that leads them to ruin."69

This monograph will deal specifically with the role of *pathos* in the book of Jude, in order to show the importance of interpreting a biblical passage. Therefore, the role of *pathos* in Judaism during the New Testament time surely plays a significant part in understanding the *pathos* of New Testament passages. Undoubtedly, the Hebrews of that time are influenced greatly in their

---

65 Elliott, *Faithful Feelings*, 81.
66 R. S. Childs, *Introduction to the Old Testament as Scripture* (Philadelphia: Fortress Press, 1979), 278.
67 Elliott, *Faithful Feelings*, 82.
68 Ibid., 83.
69 Ibid., 103.

understanding of *pathos* by the Hellenism that affected Hebrew culture. Greek philosophical schools certainly informed a great deal of the Hebrew system of education at that time. Elliott says, "They took the well-thought-out ideas from the (Greek) philosophers as a matter of course and integrated them with their Jewish beliefs. Most often, this was not a good match and their writings on the matter were not logically consistent with the Old Testament."[70]

The influence of Hebrew culture upon Scripture provides help for our understanding of *pathos* interpretation of biblical passages. However, this monograph does not view this as the determinative factor in *pathos* interpretation. Though helpful, this monograph asserts that the Holy Spirit's inspiration provides the crucial and guiding key to adequate exegesis of *pathos* in Scripture interpretation.

BIBLICAL BACKGROUND

To read the Bible and not be aware that *pathos* (emotional mood) plays a vital role in proper understanding of the text requires effort! Whether consciously or not, awareness that Bible passages carry emotional meaning seems to be a part of most who exegete and proclaim Scripture. Although too often exegetes and preachers may not adequately address the emotional message in a biblical passage.

Hollifield counsels preachers to give careful attention to passage *pathos*:

> The Bible pulsates with emotion. Few sermons that attempt to expound a biblical text ever seem to lay a finger on its pulse. Often the emotions provoked by the typical sermon, whether topical, textual, or expository, fail to grow out of the text. The preacher who desires to exegete the Scriptures accurately and attractively can do so by giving greater attention to the emotional dimension. The inspired text itself can establish the parameters for the emotional content and delivery of the sermon, meaning that the emotions of the sermon are informed by careful exegesis.[71]

---

70 Elliott, *Faithful Feelings*, 121.
71 Gregory K. Hollifield, "Expository Preaching That Touches the Heart,"

There may be differences in one's reading of biblical emotions relative to emotional responses today. Spencer says, "An important task for interpreters is explaining how biblical emotions differ from present perceptions of them."[72] Not only is this true, but the emotions elicited in the Bible are also very different from those in the culture surrounding its composition at that time. Fortenbaugh indicates, for example, that Aristotle doesn't seem to have any corresponding emotion to the Christian virtue of mercy. He states that, for Aristotle . . . that feeling (of) pity is viewed as "a non-practical emotion."[73]

As to current thinking about jealousy versus the perception of the same emotion in the Hebrew Bible, Fortenbaugh is helpful. He explains that the Hebrew Bible thinks about jealousy in terms of someone possessing something they should not rightfully have. In our current consumer cultural atmosphere, people are rewarded for obtaining something they may not be supposed to get, and are praised for their greed.[74]

Hollifield elaborates on the subject of biblical emotions. He says, "The Bible pulsates with emotion."[75] To ignore this crucial fact of biblical interpretation is to render the Bible a dead, heartless, and impotent book. Such interpretation may have the content of biblical passage correct but totally miss the spirit and heart of the passage.

A sampling of the emotional mood of Old and New Testament genre will be given in the following section of this monograph. Obviously, an in-depth analysis of the *pathos* in either Testament would be far beyond the scope of our efforts. An attempt to sample the emotional content of a few of the genre in the two Testaments will be attempted by this author.

Preaching, http://www.preaching.com/resources/articles/11549461/(accessed March 7, 2019).

72   Spencer, *Mixed Feelings and Vexed Passions*, 57.

73   Fortenbaugh, *Aristotle on Emotion*, 83.

74   Spencer, *Mixed Feelings and Vexed Passions*, 57-58. Spencer's discussion of this point explains the difference between emotions today that are clearly different from those found in the Bible.

75   Hollifield, "Expository Preaching That Touches the Heart," 18.

Introduction: Historical Background

Old Testament *Pathos*

The narrative sections of the Old Testament are rich in *pathos*. Virtually every emotion known to man may be found in the narrative portions of Old Testament Scripture. A careful reading of Old Testament narrative passages reveal abundant examples of the emotional content found therein.

In a prior devotional time, this writer read a series of chapters in 1 Samuel that have to do with David's experiences with King Saul. When David returns from his conquest of Goliath, the people respond to him with "singing and dancing . . . with shouts of joy" (1 Sam 18:6). From this point on, all Scripture references will be from the Christian Standard Bible (CSB) unless otherwise noted. The emotions of joy, elation, and happiness because of David's victory over a fearsome enemy are apparent.

Such celebration does not receive the joyful response by at least one person. King Saul "watched David jealously from that day forward" (1 Sam 18:9). On the next day King Saul's jealousy takes another downward step. In a fit of anger, he "began to rave . . ." (18:10-11) and threw a sword at David. Frightful emotions of jealousy, anger, and outburst manifest themselves.

The poetical books of the Old Testament carry their readers through every conceivable emotion. David's prayer of confession in Psalm 51 is a case in point. Coming to God in a deeply emotional and intimate way, David records his repentance for his shameful adultery with Bathsheba. He begins this penitent psalm with a plea for grace and compassion: "Be gracious to me, God, . . . according to your abundant compassion" (Ps 51:1). A cursory reading of that plea reveals emotions of deep sorrow and repentance. Toward the end of the Psalm he expresses his brokenness and humility before God: "You will not despise a broken and humbled heart, God" (Ps 51:17b). Emotions of brokenness and humility are apparent from David's words.

The Old Testament prophetic books vibrate with emotion. The book of Jonah, which is also narrative in nature, shows all kinds of emotional tonal quality. We sense Jonah's refusal to do God's will in chapter one, his desperate prayer for deliverance in chapter two, then his willingness to preach to hated enemies in chapter three. In all of these scenes, we see the reluctant prophet experiencing disobedience, fear, begging for mercy to glad, judgment-filled proclamation to hated enemies. Jonah 4 contains a variety of emotional moods by Jonah. His emotions swirl like a destructive storm in the prophet's heart. He moves from being "greatly displeased . . . (being) furious" at God's relinquished judgment toward wicked Nineveh to being "greatly pleased" with a gourd, to prayer for death and obvious indifference to God's compassion for sinners (Jonah 4:1, 4, 9, 10-11). Jonah's flood of contrasting emotions will not be missed by the observant Bible interpreter.

New Testament *Pathos*

The study of *pathos* in the New Testament does not lend itself to simplicity. Elliott says about the difficulty, "Here we see some of the complexity of the study of emotion in the New Testament. The syntax and style alone can show emotion. This kind of analysis has remained in the background of our study . . . The role of emotion within the New Testament is a key factor in understanding the early (church) community."[76]

Pathos in the New Testament differs from the Greek culture of its time. This is demonstrated by the use of the word for *pathos* itself. Hellenistic philosophers generally used the word in a generic sense. Elliott points out that Philo used the word *pathos* (pathe) over 400 times with the idea of something destructive in need of conquest.[77] In contrast, the New Testament has a wider range of meanings, both positive as well as negative.

Our survey of New Testament *pathos* at this point has more to do with deciphering the emotional mood of passages found in the various genre of our New Testament than it does with just the meaning of the words. The narrative sections of the New Testament are rich in emotional content and yield much interpretative fruit to the diligent exegete.

Think of the *pathos* of the passage recorded in Luke 24 about the resurrection walk of Jesus with the two disciples. As these disciples walk along the Emmaus road, they are discussing recent events in Jerusalem. Luke records they were "discussing and arguing" about them (Luke 24:13-15). The *pathos* of the scene can't be missed. Surely disappointment, puzzlement, anxiety, and strong

---

76 Elliott, *Faithful Feelings*, 237.
77 Ibid., 134.

Introduction: Historical Background

emotions expressed by their differing opinions are easily seen. As the living Lord Jesus joined them in their journey, He asks them about their disputed conversation. They stop their walking and "looked discouraged" (Luke 24:16). The emotion of unmet expectations oozes from the statement. Move forward in the narrative: "But we were hoping . . ." (Luke 24:21). The *pathos* of unfulfilled desire can't be missed. Fast forward. When the living Savior reveals Himself to the two at the table in the breaking of bread, they declare "weren't our hearts burning within us . . . ?" (Luke 24:32). Abundant *pathos* presents itself from a stirred, warmed heart inside them. Hogan and Reid say about that experience, "Emotions and feelings are at the very center of our relationship with God and one another."[78]

Next, move to the book of the Revelation which, though there are elements of letter and other genre, the primary category of apocalyptic provides the best classification of the Revelation. As in other sections of the New Testament, the plentitude of passage *pathos* in the Revelation prevents a total analysis of all the examples. As will be suggested in conclusion, this kind of work needs to be done in order to give a complete analysis of biblical passages. A few examples should give the kinds of emotions one experiences in this apocalyptic book. John hears the call in chapter five for the book sealed on the inside and outside to be opened. Finding no one in heaven, in the earth, nor under the earth capable of doing so, John says, "I wept and wept because no one was found worthy to open the scroll or even to look in it" (Rev 5:5). Great sorrow cannot not be missed in John's words. When the worthy Lord Jesus Christ takes the scroll and opens it, the twenty-four living creatures "sang a new song" (Rev 5:9). The scene moves from John's sorrow on earth to great joy in heaven over the worthiness of Christ to open the scroll.

On the closing page of the Revelation, the Lord Jesus three times announces, "Look, I am coming soon!" (Rev 22:7, 12, 20). Emotions of victory, celebration, and anticipation burst forth. John's reply, "Amen! Come Lord Jesus!" (Rev 22:20), gives clear evidence of great joy and anticipation in response to the promise of the Lord Jesus.

For purposes of this monograph, the New Testament letters demand our evaluation of emotional content. The New Testament letters have a goal or theme that drives them. Though heavily didactic, strong emotions mani-

---

78 Hogan and Reid, *Connecting with the Congregation*, 71.

fest themselves within the arguments, personal conflicts, and other aspects of New Testament letters. Several illustrations from Paul's letter to the Galatians demonstrate this to be true. At the very outset, the interpreter senses Paul has a definite emotional mood. While his normal approach involves words of commendation to a particular church or person, Galatians barely moves beyond the opening praise to God for His grace and peace, until Paul directly confronts the church with the pronouncement that their churches have "so quickly (turned) to a different gospel . . ." (Gal 1:6). The emotional mood is one of astonishment, and discontent, to the point that Paul chides them.

Further, Paul mentions his conflict with the apostle Peter. In discussing their confrontation such words as "opposed . . . condemned . . . withdrew . . . feared . . . hypocrisy . . ." (Gal 2:11-14). These are emotion-laden words. Merely reading them indicates the strong emotions they represent in the confrontation. In Galatians 2:4, Paul makes mention of "false brothers (who had) infiltrated our ranks to spy . . ." Paul clearly displays discontent, disturbance, and distain for them. Even in the category of letters, the thorough Bible interpreter must not miss the *pathos* found there.

The brief survey of *pathos* in the Old and New Testaments is not exhaustive, but suggestive. The purpose of this brief section of the monograph is to point toward the specific importance of the book of Jude which will be the proving ground for the central argument of this monograph. This chapter maintains, in the words of Elliott, "It is important to emphasize the consistent presence of links between cognition and emotion that appear in the New Testament."[79] Such linkage provides crucial background to the argument of the thesis that will be set forth in the chapters relative to the importance of *pathos* as illustrated in the book of Jude.

---

79 Elliott, *Faithful Feelings*, 235.

Chapter Two

Pathos and Preaching

"Why are you so mad? Who are you mad with?" Those words rushed out of the lips of Dr. Friednitz Brodnitz, the eminent otolaryngologist in New York City. Dr. Brodnitz achieved a great deal of acclaim because of his success in solving problems of the vocal cords experienced by a large number of opera singers and actors. And also preachers. Dr. Stephen Olford, who experienced vocal difficulties, referred me to him because of the vocal issues that threatened to hamper my ministry.

In response to Brodnitz's directive, several of my message tapes were sent to him. Thus, the questions at the beginning of this chapter. The questions astonished me. The skilled doctor pointed out I was preaching about the love of God and doing so with anger in my voice. The criticism hit the mark. Angry indeed at several difficult people in my congregation. The words expressed with hostile emotions didn't match the tenderness of the passages about God's love. The young preacher came face to face with an oft-used statement: What the preacher says is important. How he says it is also important.

Beyond question those who preach must be called and have an anointing to do so. No doubt, either, that there are some who seem to be especially gifted to preach. Yet, increasing skill in preaching may be developed. Erasmus reportedly said, "If elephants can be trained to dance, lions to play and leopards to hunt, surely priests can be taught to preach.[80]" In that vein, preachers may further be trained to look for and communicate biblical passage *pathos*.

---

80 John R. W. Stott, *Between Two Worlds* (Grand Rapids: William B. Eerd-

THE VITAL ROLE OF *PATHOS* IN A COMPLETE TEXT-DRIVEN INTERPRETATION OF THE BOOK OF JUDE

Each of Aristotle's three elements in rhetorical persuasion must be a feature in the delivery of a text-driven message. The careful student will see often that the purpose of biblical preaching is persuasion toward life-changing decisions for Jesus Christ. Paul summarizes the biblical thrust toward persuasion as the goal of preaching quite well when he says, "Therefore, since we know the fear of the Lord, we try to persuade people" (2 Cor 5:11). Paige Patterson compares preaching to the flight of an airplane. *Ethos* suggests the well-trained, trusted pilot. *Logos* calls attention to the cargo the plane transports. Then, he says, "*Pathos* would be the trim on the wings and tail of the plane. All of this that is to be used of God must be borne along on the zephyr winds of the Holy Spirit."[81]

This particular chapter ties *pathos* to the preaching endeavor. The failure to include *pathos* in preaching pericopes of Scripture constitutes one of the areas that needs careful attention in biblically sound proclamation. The divorce of biblical passion from the preaching assignment renders the pulpit dull, boring, and actually unfaithful. The separation of appeals to the mental reception of a message and an audience's response to its emotional message produces just such an undesirable effect.

The words of D. Martyn Lloyd-Jones serve as a corrective to that temptation: "We tend to lose our balance and to become over-intellectual, indeed almost to despise the element of feeling and emotion. We are such learned men, we have such a great grasp of the Truth, that we tend to despise feeling."[82] This writer sees the tendency in many circles at present. Lloyd-Jones goes further:

> Emotion is regarded as something indecent. My reply to all that, once more is simply to say that if you contemplate the glorious truths that are committed to our charge as preachers without being moved by them there is something defective in your spiritual eyesight . . . I fear that many people today in their reaction against excesses and emotionalism

---

mans Publishing Company, 1982), 213.

81 Akin, Allen, and Matthews, *Text-Driven Preaching*, 35.

82 Dr. Martyn Lloyd-Jones, *Preachers and Preaching* (Grand Rapids: Zondervan, 2011), 106.

put themselves into a position in which, in the end, they are virtually denying truth.[83]

This monograph doesn't argue for just any kind of emotion in preaching. Of course, mere emotional preaching may be exciting and stirring, but missing the emotion of the particular biblical passion itself risks missing the content as well. Biblical passion must be prominent. As shall be demonstrated, the emotions of a passage impact the meaning. The same God who inspired the content of Scripture also inspired its *pathos*. To miss this carries the risk that the one who attempts to preach a biblical passage may actually miss the Holy Spirit's intention as to its meaning.

Jonathan Edwards sets forth the matter helpfully: "If a minister has light without heat . . . he may gratify itching ears, and fill the heads of his people with empty notions; but it will not be very likely to reach their hearts . . . if, on the other hand, he be driven on with . . . vehement heat, without light, he will be likely to kindle the unhallowed flame in his people. . . ."[84]

THE EXEGETICAL LINK BETWEEN *PATHOS* AND PREACHING

The words we say make a difference. How we say those words also makes a difference. The tone we use when speaking a sentence can be crucial in the interpretation of those words. Shift the tonal emphasis of this statement—"What do you intend to do about it?" Place the emphasis like this—"**What** do you intend," or "What do you **intend**," or "What do **you** . . ." One can easily see how different volume and inflection can turn the question to a simple inquiry, a request for a plan of action, or an accusation that one needs to take action in a matter that may not be appropriate. Emotional communication may be as crucial or even more so than our mere words when seeking to get a message to people.

---

83   Lloyd-Jones, *Preachers and Preaching,* 107-108.

84   Jonathan Edwards, "The True Excellency of a Gospel Minister," in *The Works of Jonathan Edwards*, Vol. 2 (Edinburgh: Banner of Truth, 1974), 958.

THE VITAL ROLE OF *PATHOS* IN A COMPLETE TEXT-DRIVEN INTERPRETATION OF THE BOOK OF JUDE

Do you recall certain sermons more than others? There are indeed sermons that are forgettable. This author confesses to a multitude of those! Other sermons stay with us indefinitely. They stirred us and moved us in the depth of our being. Surely, the biblical truth plays a key, primary role. But, also, deep down within our hearts, released emotional springs flooded our hearts with lifechanging stirrings. For this reason, Adam Dooley says, "We simply cannot afford to ignore the emotive consequences of sermon *pathos*."[85]

During the years of this writer's preaching ministry, several shifts in the landscape of homiletics transpired. In earlier years, the propositional truths of the Bible prominently occupied the field. Then, there seemed to be a reaction to propositional preaching. Fred Craddock introduced the concept commonly called the New Homiletic. Mark Howell's Ph.D. dissertation gives a very good analysis of the movement.[86] The New Homiletic placed the importance of narrative plot and telling the story in emotional language in a central and primary position on the field of homiletics. In the course of such preaching, the listeners were to come to their own conclusions as to the meaning of a preached passage. Dooley says, "Though this type of preaching engaged listeners, its practitioners often entertained congregations with sermons in search of a text."[87] Given that many leaders in the movement were more liberal in their views on Scripture, the New Homiletic received little positive response by conservatives.

More recently the return to the actual meaning of Scripture as to its content again takes front and center on the homiletic field. With the renewed emphasis upon the inerrancy of Scripture came verse-by-verse preaching. "Let the text speak for itself," the new generation of preachers declare. The result produces a welcome return to the *logos* of Scripture.

However, there often results a tendency to move too far from the *pathos* of Scripture. There must be no jettisoning of the emotional mood in Scripture. Again, Dooley says, "Capturing the meaning of Scripture without also commu-

---

85 Vines and Dooley, *Passion in the Pulpit*, 24.

86 Mark A. Howell, "Hermeneutical Bridges and Homiletical Methods: A Comparative Analysis of the New Homiletic and Expository Preaching Theory 1970-1995." A dissertation presented to the faculty of Southeastern Baptist Theological Seminary, Wake Forest, North Carolina, 1999.

87 Vines and Dooley, *Passion in the Pulpit*, 25.

nicating its heart falls short of the divine mandate to preach the Word."[88] There must be no either/or; there must be both/and.

We return at this juncture to Aristotle and his helpful categories of *logos*, *pathos*, and *ethos*. These rhetorical categories still serve communicators well. Perhaps almost all will agree that *logos*, the content of a sermon, is primary in Scripture's interpretation and proclamation. *Ethos*, specifically the credibility of the preacher in the proclamation setting, continues to occupy a vital role in effective preaching of Scripture.

Further, there must be no neglect of the concept of passion in a faithful handling of Scripture. This writer does not intend to convey the concept of merely the preacher's emotion in the course of preaching a Scripture passage. Unfortunately, this seems to be the thrust of most contemporary discussions of preaching *pathos*.

The underlying assumption of this monograph moves toward the emotional mood of the text of Scripture, not that of the preacher. While the subject of the preacher's personal *pathos* must be addressed, this monograph emphasizes that the preacher needs to communicate the emotional tone of his textual pericope, not his own. Dooley refers to this as "the emotional exegetical link." He avows: "In a preaching context, this requires those who handle the Word to not only embody the emotional tone of their text, but also to elicit the same from the congregation."[89]

Full and complete biblical exposition must include interpreting the Bible passage in terms of how what is said in addition to what is said. Hollifield explains it thusly: "The preacher who desires to exegete Scriptures accurately and attractively can do so by giving greater attention to the emotional dimension. The inspired text itself can establish the parameters for the emotional content and delivery of the sermon, meaning that (a comprehension of) the emotions of the sermon are informed by careful exegesis."[90] The necessity of this exegetical approach will be demonstrated in the latter discussions relative to preparing a series of text-driven messages from the book of Jude.

---

88 Vines and Dooley, *Passion in the Pulpit*, 25.
89 Ibid., 26.
90 Hollified, "Expository Preaching That Touches the Heart," 18.

THE VITAL ROLE OF *PATHOS* IN A COMPLETE TEXT-DRIVEN INTERPRETATION OF THE BOOK OF JUDE

Extremes must be avoided in adequate biblical exegesis. Hershael York calls them factoid sermons leading to knowledge, but little life change. Or sermons that stir, but do not stir on the basis of the application of Bible truth to living experience. [91]

As in every approach to Scripture, balance must be maintained. Dooley says: "Conservatives that no one can/will listen to may speak the truth, but they are not preaching. Likewise, liberals who skillfully engage their audience but have nothing of substance to say aren't preaching either. We need *logos* and *pathos* in order to carry out our charge to preach the Word."[92]

All who preach do so from a definite cultural setting. This writer does so also. In my setting, passionate preaching determined whether or not the preacher really preached! Too often, however, this meant loud, breathless, exhausting preaching. Such a cultural atmosphere has a long history. Quintilian has an informative and amusing evaluation of overwrought speakers: "Such pleaders try by their delivery to gain the reputation of speaking with energy, for they bawl on every occasion. (They use every opportunity) to clap the hands together, to stamp the foot on the ground, to strike the thigh, the breast, and the forehead with the hand . . ."[93]

This monograph makes the necessary distinction between wrought up emotional preaching and preaching with text-driven *pathos*. The latter leads to what may be termed heart preaching. The psalmist declares, "Deep calls unto deep . . ." (Psalm 42:7a). Those who listen to preachers will not be moved correctly until "we convey to them what our passage of Scripture has stirred within us."[94] This will be achieved as the preacher assimilates into his personality and deepest soul the thrust of the biblical passage. Jim Shaddix gives a helpful hypothetical suggestion, "Maybe Christians—and especially preachers—should consider the culture with a different T-shirt. On the front it

---

91 Hershael York and Bert Decker, *Preaching with Bold Assurance* (Nashville: Broadman & Holman Publishing, 2003), 12-15. This is a very helpful contribution to the current study.

92 Vines and Dooley, *Passion in the Pulpit,* 30.

93 Patricia Bizzell and Bruce Herzberg, eds., quoted in *The Rhetorical Tradition,* 2nd ed. (Boston: Bedford/St. Martin, 2001), 382.

94 Vines and Dooley, *Passion in the Pulpit,* 34.

could simply read, 'It's not about me . . . And on the back it could read, 'It's all about Him!'"[95]

To that end several premises must be followed. First, seek to find the inspired *pathos* of every biblical text. Second, realize this is essential if correct interpretation of the text results. Third, letting that textual *pathos* guide in a proper understanding and application of the text will produce a full and complete exegesis of the text.

Adequately communicating with an audience occupies a prominent place in the preaching endeavor. The importance of that needs no elaboration. This must not be elevated to such a place that the Bible's message receives only background emphasis. One may so emphasize good communication that Bible *pathos* takes a backseat to that of the preacher. Ignoring Bible *pathos* and emphasizing that of the preacher may be stirring, but lacking in correct and complete text-driven emphasis. Dooley says, "Elevating the mood or personality of the preacher often distorts an accurate understanding of all that a biblical writer seeks to communicate in the Scripture."[96]

This writer reflects back over sixty-five plus years of pulpit ministry with clearer eyes. Though not fully aware of all the intellectual underpinnings of preaching passage *pathos*, it received emphasis. These words from *Passion in the Pulpit* provide some insight into what transpired. "When I preached on the sublimity of God's creation in Genesis one, I preached the passion of the text with wonder-filled words and eyes bursting with amazement. I preached the lament psalms with sorrow-tinged vocal delivery and physical indication of heartache."

As previously indicated, the writer regards such preaching as heart preaching. George Whitfield's preaching fits well into that category. Stout, in his interesting book, *The Divine Dramatist*, says that Whitefield "became" the characters of the Bible he presented. When he preached on Zacchaeus, he became the little man climbing up and sliding down the sycamore tree. Stout says, "He was not 'acting' as he preached so much as he was exhibiting a one-to-one correspondence between his inner passions and the biblical saints he embod-

---

95 Jim Shaddix, *The Passion-Driven Sermon* (Nashville: Broadman and Holman, 2003), 29.

96 Vines and Dooley, *Passion in the Pulpit,* 28.

ies."⁹⁷ Following this quotation by Stout, the author adds, "Whether consciously or unconsciously, Whitefield took the *pathos* of Scripture and made it real in his own heart. That is heart preaching!"⁹⁸

John Piper argues for passionate preaching: "Brothers, we must let the river run deep. This is a plea for passion in the pulpit, passion in prayer, passion in conversation. It is not a plea for thin, whipped-up emotionalism . . . It is a plea for deep feelings in worthy forms from God-besotted hearts and minds."

To this the writer gives hearty agreement, with this caveat. The emotion conveyed by the preacher to the audience must not be his own, but that of the preaching passage. Kim's statement conveys this necessity: "It is very true that preachers should have passion in their heart for the truth and their congregation, but if preachers' concern is only passion for them, it is unavoidable that they will fail to see and deliver the biblical *pathos* designed by the author."⁹⁹ Only as the preacher makes the *pathos* of Scripture his own can he adequately convey that Scripture emotion to the listeners.

Dooley provides a helpful three-step cycle to assist the preacher or teacher in developing a text-driven sermon. The proper place of *pathos* in the cycle takes its place. First, interpret the *logos*. The exegete must begin with interpretation of the *logos* of the passage. The content of the passage must always be the first consideration in the work of exegesis. Second, identify the *pathos*. Taking advantage of a number of tools that will be given later in this monograph enables the preacher to discover the emotional mood of the passage at hand. Third, internalize the *ethos*. The words of the preaching text must be wholeheartedly embraced by the preacher. This approach lends itself to well-rounded interpretation and application. Dooley says, "Persuasion happens when we explain the meaning (*logos*), embody the mood (*pathos*), and embrace the *ethos*."¹⁰⁰

---

97   Harry S. Stout, *The Divine Dramatist: George Whitefield and the Rise of Modern Evangelicalism* (Grand Rapids: Eerdmans, 1991), 106.

98   Vines and Dooley, *Passion in the Pulpit*, 149.

99   Kim, "The Right Use of Biblical *Pathos*," 11.

100 Vines and Dooley, *Passion in the Pulpit*, 32.

DANGER:
PREACHER'S *PATHOS*, NOT PASSAGE

Thus far the axiom is suggested that the *pathos* of a biblical passage, not that of the speaker, must be conveyed to the listeners. This will be maintained throughout the monograph in various ways. There will be tools given to assist one in discerning the emotional tone of a passage as well as its content. Using the book of Jude as the laboratory, this insight will be illustrated to demonstrate that passage *pathos* is necessary to an adequate, Spirit-intended interpretation of the same.

At this juncture, a warning must be emphasized again. Care must be taken that not the preacher's *pathos*, but that of the biblical passage being proclaimed is conveyed. However well meaning, if the preacher does not avoid this danger, the textual *pathos* will not be adequately transmitted to the listeners. Helm illustrates this danger with an interesting illustration. He says that preachers may "use the Bible the way a drunk uses a lamppost . . . we superimpose our deeply held passions, plans and perspectives on the biblical text. When we do so, the Bible becomes little more than a support for what we have to say."[101]

In a recent book, *Passion in the Pulpit*, this writer and Adam Dooley devote an entire chapter with the goal to avoid this danger. Dooley spends a good bit of time discussing the popular definition of preaching endorsed by a host of teachers, that is drawn from the legendary pastor, Phillips Brooks. Few students of sermon preparation have failed to hear or read his definition of preaching as the communication of "truth through personality." Though drawing virtual unanimous support from practitioners of preaching, Dooley challenges this definition. (For a full discussion, chapter two of *Passion in the Pulpit* should be consulted.) This famous definition of preaching first appears in his Yale Lectures on Preaching in 1877.

Taking the lead from Charles Fuller, Dooley warns the definition is inadequate for preaching, placing more emphasis on the preacher's personality than the truth of the Bible.[102]

---

101   David R. Helm, *1 and 2 Peter and Jude* (Wheaton: Crossway, 2008), 25-26.
102   Charles Fuller, "The Trouble with 'Truth through Personality,'" in Phillips Brooks, *Incarnation and the Evangelical Boundaries of Preaching* (Eugene, OR:

The view taken by Dooley and Fuller has not been widely endorsed. The author of this monograph doesn't totally reject the thesis of their argument but raises some issues that perhaps need further investigation. One cannot be totally sure that Brooks had an inferior view of regarding Scripture as the Word of God. Warren Wiersbe quoted Brooks' definition of preaching favorably. Wiersbe, however, does acknowledge the doctrinal problems exhibited by Brooks. He says, that Brooks "was a 'Christian humanist.' Brooks emphasized Christ's incarnation, not His death and atonement for sin."[103]

However, at the conclusion of that discussion Wiersbe makes reference to a further lecture Brooks delivered at the Yale Divinity School in 1878. He quotes Brooks from that lecture: "Let us rejoice with one another that in a world where there are a great many good and happy things for men to do, God has given us the best and happiest, and made us preachers of *His truth* [emphasis added]."[104] Did this indicate an interpretation of what he meant by his "truth through personality" definition? Did it indicate a new commitment to the Bible as the inerrant Word of God? We cannot be sure. The now deceased Brooks cannot clarify his definitions for us.

Having stated some minor reservations in the previous paragraphs, the views of Dooley and Brooks serve at least as a helpful caution for us. Given the times in which Brooks lived and the apparent influence of an unhealthy romanticism on Brooks, today's preachers must at least be careful. Though Brooks does affirm Christian orthodoxy as to the Trinity and the deity of Christ, there seems to be good evidence from his own writing that he denies the inerrancy of Scripture and possibility the substitutionary atonement of Christ.

Further research should be done to aid a clearer understanding of Brooks's views and the dangers of personality-driven preaching rather than text-driven preaching. Whatever view one takes, the dangers of personality-driven preaching must be heeded. To convey the *pathos* of the preacher's personality rather than that of the text renders the text somewhat meaningless and jettisons the communication of the textual truth.

Wipf and Stock, 2010), 27.

103   Warren Wiersbe, *Walking With Giants* (Grand Rapids: Baker, 1976), 83.
104   Ibid., 87.

Dooley correctly affirms, "At minimum, the elevation of personality to equal footing with truth is troubling. . . . Why should a sermon declare the preacher? For most, doing so would distract from, rather than point to the truth at hand."[105] To do so makes the authority of preaching inherent in the preacher himself. The preacher, not Scripture, becomes the criteria of deciding truth. Thus, the admonition of our selected book of Jude to "earnestly contend for the faith that was delivered to the saints once for all"(Jude 3) loses its authority for the would-be exegete and messenger of God's inerrant, revealed truth. Again, Dooley declares: "When human personality is the source of revelation, uniformity of faith is not only impossible but also problematic."[106]

Scripture is abundantly clear that preaching must be a faithful declaration of "Thus saith the Lord," and not "Thus saith the preacher." Just a few examples should suffice. Paul admonishes ". . . you received the Word of God that you heard from us, you welcomed it not as a human message, but as it truly is, the Word of God . . ." (1 Thess 2:13). He declares, "For we are not proclaiming ourselves but Jesus Christ as Lord, and ourselves as your servants for Jesus's sake" (2 Cor 4:5).

This does not minimize in any way the necessity of the preacher to use his personality as the Spirit-yielded vehicle through which the Holy Spirit communicates the *logos* and *pathos* of divine revelation. Of course, the inherent authority of what the Bible says ultimately directs us as to what to say. This is prior to and above whatever aspects of our personality may be used by the Holy Spirit to convey the Word of God. But this author is in solid agreement with Dooley that "your unique personality can, and should, convey your content, but it should not create it."[107]

The danger of preaching the passion of the preacher rather than the *pathos* of Scripture may be avoided by one clear-cut understanding. We will avoid this danger as long as and to the extent that we understand that we stand under the authority of Scripture, not over it. Though, for different reasons than Brooks's, there is the danger that today's interpreters and proclaimers may unconsciously place more emphasis upon preaching with their own passion

---

105 Vines and Dooley, *Passion in the Pulpit*, 39.
106 Ibid., 41.
107 Ibid., 42.

than that of Scripture. This seems to be the tendency of many modern appeals for passionate preaching. If this occurs, the essential ingredient of *pathos* in preaching goes unexpounded and fails to give Scripture the full depth, width, and height found therein. Rather, what should occur? Truth (the inerrant truth of God's Word) through personality (one that is regenerated and fully yielded to the truth of Scripture) should serve as the two driving forces as we preach with the right *logos* (content) and the right *pathos* (emotion). It is only insofar as the preacher correctly reflects the emotional mode of the Bible passage he declares that he will correctly communicate to his listeners the meaning of the passage.

Manipulation vs. Motivation

In addition to the danger that one's own *pathos* rather than the *pathos* of a passage may be prominent in the preaching event, there is an additional danger. Dooley says, "If the ditch of exegetical inaccuracy rests on one side of the sermonic highway, the ditch of unscrupulous manipulation awaits on the other."[108] The ultimate intention of text-driven preaching is to exalt the God of Scripture and to persuade the listeners toward decisions that will result in their own good and the glory of God.

The question arises: Just how may this kind of persuasion for the good of people and the glory of God be achieved? A distinction must be made between an ethically appropriate motivation and a manipulation unworthy of the gospel. Unethical methods of persuasion render the message questionable and the speaker's *ethos* less than credible. Paul declares that preaching God's Word requires that it has a negative and a positive facet: "My speech and my preaching were not with persuasive words of wisdom but a demonstration of the Spirit's power, so that your faith might not be based on human wisdom but on God's power" (1 Cor 2:4-5).

Paul's words clearly set forth the principle that motive in preaching should always be primary. They strongly assert that our use of persuasive means must come with the intention to motivate our listeners in God-honoring ways, not manipulate them with questionable intent. This goal will only be adequate-

---

108 Vines and Dooley, *Passion in the Pulpit*, 49.

ly achieved when the motivation comes from the text of Scripture, not other means of persuasion.

Rhetoric has as its purpose to employ all acceptable means to persuade an audience toward a desired course of action. As previously noted, Aristotle's three means of persuasion, *ethos*, *logos*, and *pathos*, helpfully work toward that goal. Persuasion must not be in the category of giving advice concerning certain behavioral patterns. Text-driven preaching with the intention of motivation cannot be equated with the numerous advertisements one receives for a brand of soap that suggest to us that the product will make one smell better and be more pleasing to be around! Suggestion doesn't necessarily produce correct motivation.

Nor does the kind of persuasion this writer has in mind involve bullying people into a course of action. Persuasion, if in the proper ethical mode, acknowledges and respects the right of listeners to hear and heed or hear and reject the appeal that encounters them. In *Passion in the Pulpit*, this writer illustrated the point by reference to a beloved evangelist who preached fervently on the reality of hell. His proper biblical persuasion resulted from his belief—"I really believe there is a hell, and I don't want anyone to go there."[109]

Those who preach the Bible must carefully examine their motives in seeking the response from an audience they desire. Is the purpose merely a number of decisions? Large crowds down an aisle? Does the motive involve more notches on one's evangelical gun? Such manipulation surely does not honor the Christ who is to be preached and falls short of a worthy motivation of audiences toward God-honoring decisions.

Unfortunately, more than one preacher has used the pulpit as a whipping post to get back at a troublesome church member. Some even use the pulpit to browbeat and drive people toward goals that may be worthy in themselves, but unworthy ultimately. The preacher must carefully evaluate his own motives that cause him to say what he intends to say in his message.

The whole concept of preaching the *pathos* of a biblical passage serves as a solution to the dilemma of manipulative preaching. One should seek the *pathos* of the particular text from which one preaches. Dooley says, "The ultimate good is helping listeners to feel the emotive design of the Bible . . . By

---

109 Vines and Dooley, *Passion in the Pulpit*, 60.

exposing the glory of God within the *logos* and *pathos* of our preaching passage, we persuade in the flow of the Spirit's design rather than our own fallen strategies."[110]

Biblical persuasion may be defined in a positive manner. Dooley's definition informs, "Biblical persuasion can be defined as: Utilizing means to seek the desired, voluntary response revealed within the Bible's *logos* and *pathos* in an effort to seek the glory of God and the spiritual benefit of an audience."[111] This helpful definition may well serve as a guide toward preaching that motivates and does not manipulate.

The preacher's task must always be to seek to persuade based on the persuasive intent of Scripture. This should free the preacher to preach with all the *logos* and *pathos* contained in the selected passage. The emotional mode of the passage will lead the preacher to engage whatever emotions necessary in the course of the preacher's message to achieve the desired end of Scripture, not that of the preacher. To do so indicates that the preacher is being true to the *pathos* of the biblical passage as well as its *logos*. Just as we consciously develop our sermon to convey the *logos* of the text, so we must employ acceptable means to transmit its *pathos* through the preacher to the listeners. There should be no hesitancy to use whatever emotions one desires so long as they are taken from the Scripture passage.

To gather up the main thrust of this section, the goal must be to understand that the "way" we preach our message is important, but also "why" we say it is also important. In *Passion in the Pulpit*, this writer uses the example of Satan's manipulation of Eve in the garden of Eden. Satan used a wide variety of manipulative methods to move Eve to improper decisions. Satan's motive? "To cause Eve to sin, followed by her husband, Adam, followed by the whole human race. Indeed, the motive is the real test as to manipulation or persuasion."[112]

When text-driven preachers preach, our listeners "should not only be mentally stimulated by our message (*logos*); they must also be emotionally stabbed by it (*pathos*). We must tap the secret springs of their hearts so that

---

110 Vines and Dooley, *Passion in the Pulpit*, 55.
111 Ibid., 51.
112 Ibid., 57.

they will act upon the biblical truths presented to them."[113] In well-rounded text-driven preaching, our motivation must be to bring people to faith in Christ and lead those who know Christ to Christlikeness of life and behavior. With this as our motivation, whatever the emotions of a biblical passage are discovered by our careful study may be appropriately used. "By persuasively preaching the *pathos* of Scripture as well as the *logos* of Scripture we bring glory to God and bring about good for those who hear us preach with passion in the pulpit."[114]

In the further sections of the chapter, the various tools necessary to get at the *pathos* of a text will be named and explained.

Genre as it Relates to *Pathos*

The writer of this monograph has three volumes on preaching—*Power in the Pulpit, Progress in the Pulpit,* and *Passion in the Pulpit*. The first volume *Power in the Pulpit* gives brief mention to the importance of genre in finding the emotive content of a text of Scripture. A brief discussion of genre there says, "The word genre is a French word that simply means 'form' or 'kind.' It refers to the different categories or types of literature found in the Bible."[115] Further, we indicate "the form of literary genre establishes the ground rules with which we engage the contextual evidence needed to rightly understand the meaning of any given text of Scripture."[116] Brief mention of the categories of Bible genre may also be found there.[117]

The second volume *Progress in the Pulpit* narrows the focus, giving more detail about the importance of discerning the literary genre of a Scripture passage. More specific detail about Bible genre occupies chapter five. The different genre of Scripture may be as few as five or as many as nine.[118] Steven

---

113   Vines and Dooley, *Passion in the Pulpit,* 58.
114   Ibid., 60.
115   Jerry Vines and Jim Shaddix, *Power in the Pulpit: How to Prepare and Deliver Expository Sermons,* rev. ed. (Chicago: Moody Publishers, 1999, 2017), 148.
116   Ibid., 149.
117   Ibid., 150 [see chart].
118   Steven W. Smith, *Recapturing the Voice of God: Shaping Sermons Like Scripture* (Nashville: B&H Academic, 2015), 27-29.

THE VITAL ROLE OF *PATHOS* IN A COMPLETE TEXT-DRIVEN INTERPRETATION OF THE BOOK OF JUDE

Smith's arrangement of at least nine discernable literature genres in the Bible popularizes them to three easily remembered categories. These categories are: story, poem, letter. Though these categories overlap somewhat, they give a helpful rubric for the expositor of Scripture. In spite of the overlapping, general guidelines for each category aid the expositor.

Chapter five also gives a cursory glimpse of those categories in Scripture. As to the narrative portions or story, Jeffrey Arthurs' explanation provides helpful direction: "Like the movie director using close-up and panorama, storytellers (I might add, preachers) also zoom in and out".[119]

As to poem, we point out that the poetical books follow the general rules of the Hebrew approach to poetry, giving attention to parallelism of thought rather than rhyme.

The category of letter receives brief mention in chapter five. We say, "The epistles are more didactic in style . . . we find there are many commands, couched in biblical imperatives."[120]

Volume three *Passion in the Pulpit* gives a thorough, complete discussion of the importance of discerning Scripture genre for a full-orbed exegetical analysis of a particular passage. This writer and Dooley say, "My(our) goal is not to represent a comprehensive guide for Bible interpretation, but more simply to demonstrate how a consideration of genre aids our efforts to preach with biblical *pathos*."[121]

This writer acknowledges that one may have an unconscious awareness that there are certain nuances of emotion set forth in different parts of Scripture. Some expositors seem to sense those distinctions more fully than others. But to have intellectual underpinning can do nothing but assist all exegetes and proclaimers of Scripture to a more complete awareness of the presence of *pathos* in a Scripture passage.

The discussion at this juncture of the monograph intends to indicate the interpretative necessity of knowing the literary context of a Scripture passage to

---

119 Jeffrey Arthurs, *Preaching with Variety: How to Re-create the Dynamics of Biblical Genres* (Grand Rapids: Kregel, 2007), 88.

120 Jerry Vines and Jim Shaddix. *Progress in the Pulpit: How to Grow in your Preaching* (Chicago: Moody Publishers, 2017), 89.

121 Vines and Dooley, *Passion in the Pulpit*, 63.

the end that the passage may be more clearly analyzed. This writer and Dooley say, "A careful analysis of Bible genre is the first step toward illuminating *pathos*."[122] To that end, we give consideration to eight of these categories underneath Smith's helpful three categories.

First, consider prose. This is the large category of those texts in the Bible that are conversational in nature. The Epistles fit well here. The writer and Dooley indicate that the epistle for the Philippians provides helpful understanding of prose genre. We say, "Certainly, measuring the intensity of these emotions within each preachable pericope will require additional investigation, but the overall tone of the letter is fairly obvious in large part because of the forthright nature of prose."[123]

Second, consider historical narrative. This genre finds expression in a great deal of the Old Testament and also the Gospel/Acts. More is intended than just giving the historical accounts and biographies of the major and minor players in those accounts. The Spirit-inspired authors intend more than just a rote rehearsal of events and people. This clearly may be seen in the way biblical authors, Spirit-inspired, handle biographies. Award-winning screenwriter Robert McKee says, "Biography, however, must never become a simple chronicle. That someone lived, died and did interesting things in between is of scholarly interest and no more. The biographer must . . . find the meaning of the subject's life . . . True character is revealed in the choices a human being makes under pressure."[124] These sections of Scripture lead toward proper thinking, feeling, and action. Looking at the overall genre context of a pericope of Scripture can offer a great deal of aid toward that end.

Third, consider law. This category often creates difficulty for the interpreter of Scripture. Though there can be little doubt that the moral imperatives found in this genre are God's absolutes, conveying His holiness and man's need to realize that standard, just what of the law is no longer in force and what remains as imperatives for proper living? This demands careful interpretation.

---

122   Vines and Dooley, *Passion in the Pulpit*, 65.
123   Ibid., 67.
124   Robert McKee, *Story: Substance, Structure, Style, and the Principles of Screenwriting* (New York: Harper Collins Publishers, 1997), 84.

But the category provides God's deepest emotions for the welfare of people and the strongest emotions of people seeking to obey God's commands for their life.

Fourth, consider poetry. A large portion of the Old Testament falls into this genre, the Psalms in particular. All students of poetry know its power to move the emotions, either negatively or positively. Powerful emotions receive their stimulation by the use of emotive imagery through metaphor and simile. The rhythmic flow, careful use of repetition, and liberal use of literary tropes stir one's emotions to the deepest levels of human *pathos*. As an example, consider David's prayer of confession in Psalm 51. The emotions that swirled in this man's soul flood its contents. Dooley says, "Despondency (51:1-2), transparency (vv. 3-5), longing (vv.6-12), resolve (vv. 13-15), humility and dependence (vv. 16-17) are emotional triggers within the text. . . . We forfeit a tremendous opportunity if the grief congregants feel is over David's sin rather than their own."[125]

Five, consider wisdom literature. This literature suggests the wisdom of God often in brief, but rather philosophical statements. The genre finds expression in Job, Proverbs, Ecclesiastes, and Song of Solomon. Job's moving narratives and dramatic dialogues reveal much about God's wisdom as it relates to human agonies. Proverbs floods us with emotion through brief, pointed statements. Ecclesiastes warns us as to the dangers looming due to wrong choices in life. Song of Songs overwhelms with the joys and intimacies possible within the sphere of a godly marriage.

Six, consider prophetic literature. A good portion of the Bible has to do with foretelling future events in addition to forthtelling God's message to a particular time in history. These sections of Scripture burst forth with deep emotive content. Dooley uses the book of Jonah to illustrate the contrasting emotions of God and the reluctant prophet as it relates to godless Nineveh. Jonah preached to them, but he obviously despised them. He exploded in anger when God spared them. In contrast, God responded to their repentance with remarkable compassion. God's love as revealed in Jonah must surely create emotions of conviction for lack of love for people and repentance for that lack.

Seven, consider parable. This genre normally highlights the use of stories to teach spiritual truth and condemn or commend the behavior of the readers. Sometimes the reader is left with no resolution to the matter pre-

---

125 Vines and Dooley, *Passion in the Pulpit*, 69.

sented by the story and is left to draw correct conclusions as to the meaning. Though found many times in the Old Testament, parable genre finds its best expression in the parables of Jesus. Primarily using fictitious accounts, Jesus teaches spiritual truth intended to create biblically informed emotions in those who heard him then and read them now. The parable Jesus tells of the prodigal son and the elder brother in Luke 15 vividly illustrates how this story elicits strong emotional content. Surely, one can sense the love of God for lost sinners in the picture Jesus paints of the loving father. The disastrous results of sinful choices and the marvelous road of repentance that leads the prodigal son back to the father cannot fail to stir emotions of sorrow and resolve. Finally, the anger and disdain of the elder brother surely stir within thoughtful readers emotions of conviction about an unforgiving spirit. The final scene, leaving out the response of the elder brother to the plea of the father, serves as a heart searching conclusion.

Eight, consider apocalyptic literature. One cannot miss the use of tropes to teach theological truth and look to the future. A great deal of this genre occupies the stage of the Old Testament, especially Ezekiel and Daniel. In the New Testament, though apocalyptic literature may be found in the Gospels and the Epistles, the shining example of the genre is found in the Revelation. Dramatic scenes, symbolic language, and anticipatory declarations all contribute to emotional modes of disgust at wickedness, anxiety for the impending future, but great hope for the ultimate future march across personal emotional landscapes.

Dooley summarizes the importance of knowing the genre as it relates to *pathos*: "The aforementioned considerations are not a comprehensive hermeneutical guide, but the starting line for emotional exegesis instead. Much like appreciating the differing objectives of various sports, these basic instructions will free us to celebrate the unique persuasive abilities in some passages that may be entirely absent in others."[126]

When the biblical exegete interprets the *logos* (content) of Scripture, he puts the words to the music. When he interprets the *pathos* (emotional mode) of Scripture, he puts the music to the words.

---

126   Vines and Dooley, *Passion in the Pulpit*, 73.

Vocabulary and Syntax as They Relate to *Pathos*

Words are the vehicles of thought. Without words, meaning cannot be communicated. There can be no music without notes. There can be no mathematics without numbers. Likewise, there can be no meaning without words. Words themselves also transport emotion. Perhaps the following illustration will illuminate the point. Words in Scripture may be compared to a locomotive that is pulling two separate cars. The first car is *logos* (the meaning of the words). The second one is *pathos* (the emotions conveyed by the words).

While the primacy of the *logos* meaning of biblical words has already been established, there needs to be an additional understanding that the vocabulary and syntax bring to an interpretation of a biblical pericope. They do not divulge the complete tone of said passage, but they do invariably give us the pervading rhythm of the *pathos* in the passage. This can be demonstrated in many fields of communication, as well as that of text-driven preaching.

The late Supreme Court Justice Antonin Scalia communicated *logos* and *pathos* by means of his written opinions. An originalist when it came to the interpretation of the Constitution of the United States, he communicated content and emotion by the colorful words he used. Committed to the original meaning of words, his dissent could be scathing. When the majority of the Supreme Court legalized what came to be commonly known as Obamacare, he "minced no words. He talked about 'pure applesauce' and jiggery-pokery.' He warned that the result of such rulings meant 'words have no meaning.'"[127] One can hardly miss the *pathos* of those words in addition to their *logos*!

Because this writer long has held to the inerrancy of Scripture, by logical extension this reaches to the very words of Scripture. Meaning in the Bible can only be found in an acquaintance with the meaning of the words. 1 Corinthians 2:13 clearly indicates that Spirit inspiration extends to the words of Scripture: "We also speak these things, not in words taught by human wisdom, but in those (words) taught by the Spirit

---

127 Vines and Shaddix, *Progress in the Pulpit*, 95-96.

. . ." The words of Jesus undergird this truth: "Man must not live on bread alone, but on every word that comes from the mouth of God" (Matt 4:4).

Assuming that the previous paragraph accurately states the matter, the words of Scripture (vocabulary) and their relation to one another (syntax) become all important to the expositor. Because of this conviction, the writer has spent a great deal of his preaching ministry giving attention to word study. The importance of the original languages has taken on crucial meaning as well. This conviction requires an additional step in the interpretive process which this monograph maintains has too often not been taken. Words have meaning. Words also have emotional tone.

The words of Scripture and their relation to one another possess emotions that do not escape the careful, observant exegete. As the writer moves toward the heart of this monograph, an analysis of passage *pathos* becomes vital. To accurately and fully interpret the book of Jude, the consideration of a Bible book's emotional mode in the use of the Spirit-directed vocabulary and syntax constitutes a vital component of the exercise. Careful attention will be given to the *pathos* of the words and syntax of the book of Jude in a further chapter. At this juncture, a general discussion of *pathos* in Scripture vocabulary and syntax provides necessary direction toward that endeavor.

Words create deep feeling and profound action. Those who communicate Scripture must give careful to include this facet of Scripture study. Without this, the transmission of biblical truth will lack thorough exegesis. Careful attention must be made to the idea that pulpit *pathos* must not be just any kind of emotion, whether that of the preacher or even reflecting the emotional atmosphere of the audience. The message requires thorough immersion in the emotions intended by the inerrant text of Scripture. The writer recognizes that this kind of interpretive endeavor moves some into new territory. A commitment to engage in passage *pathos* interpretation will provide many profitable and rewarding insights. One's exposition and proclamation of Scripture cannot help but be enhanced.

In *pathos* analysis of words in a Scripture passage, an important distinction must be made between two kinds of words that are found. An introduction to this kind of vocabulary and syntactical analysis may be studies in David Allen's excellent chapter "Preparing a Text-Driven Sermon" in *Text-Driven*

Preaching. Some words may be called function words. Prepositions, conjunctions, and articles are in this category. These kinds of words obtain meaning from their usage in grammar and syntax.

The field of linguistics helps us understand the importance of these function words. Function words are referred to as "discourse markers." By this is meant that they bracket off parts of a biblical passage those words and phrases that hang together. Some conjunctions are intended to be connect words, phrases or clauses that have equal status. Other conjunctions alert the reader that there is a significant development in the flow of the argument found in the text. Even these function words can deliver emotional impact. Consider the contrasting conjunction of Ephesians 2:4. "But God! . . ." (CSB). Few will escape the emotional impact of that conjunction!

Though definite articles do not always indicate *logos* and *pathos*, at times they do. In anticipating the analysis of Jude, consider the use of the definite article in "the faith" in verse 3. As to content, the article suggests that body of belief that constitutes the essentials of Christianity. As to emotional mode, the article suggests emotions such as confidence, gratitude, and determination.

More importantly, some words in a Scripture passage may be called content words. Whereas the function words may be called the mortar of language, content words are the bricks of language. These are the nouns, verbs, adjectives, and adverbs of the passage. The meaning of these words may be obtained from lexicons and usage through the years of the particular language of the text. Looking forward to this monograph's exegesis of the book of Jude, consider a few examples. Great amounts of information (*logos*) and inspiration (*pathos*) are found in the content words of Jude. For example, the verb "kept" (used five times in Jude: verses 1, 6, 13, 21). The word conveys meaning in terms of being safe from harm. A careful study of the word's uses in Jude clearly teaches that there is a keeping God does (v. 24) and a keeping believers must do (v. 21). *Pathos* is also communicated by the use of the verb "kept." As to the keeping God does (v. 24), emotions of gratitude, assurance, joy, and confidence emerge from its uses. As to the keeping believers must do (v. 21), emotions such as determination, anticipation, and dedication emerge.

The imperatives of a Scripture passage deliver deeply felt emotions also. Verbal imperatives inspire toward negative or positive kinds of activity.

The imperatives of Jude find expression in statements near the end. Some examples are: "Remember" (v. 17) and "keep yourselves" (v. 21). "Remember" can bring forth the emotion of fondness. "Keep yourselves" elicits feelings of commitment and confidence.

The writer recognizes that vocabulary and syntax in and of themselves do not always convey the *pathos* of a Scripture passage. Though they do convey its driving rhythm, other factors frequently come into play. Lesser emotions at times call attention to the primary *pathos* of a passage. Dooley illustrates this by the contrasting grief reflected by words like "despair," "disturbed," and "rejected" in Psalm 42:5, 11 and 43:2, 5 (NASB). These words serve to highlight by contrast the confident faith that the psalmist ultimately feels: "Put your hope in God!" (Ps. 42:5, 11; 43:5).[128]

Syntax comes into play by the relation of words, phrases, and clauses to one another. Also, syntax provides guidance as to the placement of certain words and phrases. The careful exegete will look not only at how a passage or a verse begins, but also how it ends. Again, looking ahead to the book of Jude provides insight. Jude doesn't begin, but rather ends with a moving doxology. After the often depressing and heart-rending assertions of Jude, the closing doxology provides for a mountaintop kind of *pathos* in Jude's epistle.

The writer at this point restates again the principle that the words of Scripture not only should inform us, but they should emotionally stab us. Charles Simeon said, "Screw the word into the minds of your hearers. A screw is the strongest of all mechanical powers . . . when it has turned a few times, scarcely any power can pull it out."[129] To add to those excellent words from Simeon: screw the *pathos* of scriptural passages into the hearts of your audience. Do this by taking the words and syntax of Scripture and correctly convey them through your own personality and delivery.

As the story goes, Mark Twain's wife, Livy, who was a devout Christian was disturbed by his use of profanity. To cause him to hear the disturbing profane words he had just used, she repeated them to him word for word. After

---

[128] Vines and Dooley, *Passion in the Pulpit,* 82.

[129] E. C. Dargan, *A History of Preaching* (New York: Hodder and Stoughton, 1912), 124ff.

a moment's silence, Twain replied, "You got the words right, Livy, but you don't know the tune."

The interpretation of the *logos* of a Scripture passage puts the words to the music. The interpretation of the *pathos* of that passage adds the music to the words. "When we preach let us make very certain that we adequately speak with the correct tune as well as the words of Scripture. The syntax and words of Scripture have a definite *pathos*."[130]

---

130 Vines and Dooley, *Passion in the Pulpit,* 90.

Chapter Three

Exegetical Summary of Jude's *Logos*

The focus of this monograph continues to zoom in closer to an analysis of passage *pathos* in the book of Jude. As indicated, Jude serves as an example of the importance of interpreting such *pathos* toward a full, complete, and well-rounded exegetical presentation and proclamation of Bible truth. With that ultimate purpose in mind, there must be awareness that there need not be a detailed examination of the empirical content of Jude.

However, a general examination of Jude's passage *logos* must precede its *pathos*. As previously stated, *logos* must always be the first step in an adequate exegesis of any biblical passage. Thus, chapter three will give a necessary summary discussion of Jude's content. Then, chapter four will move into an examination and discussion of Jude's emotional mode.

Hans Georg Gadamer and Paul Ricoeur present a systematic algorithm that proves to be expeditious to the exegete of biblical passages.[131] They talk about interpreting textual content in terms of the world behind the text and the world in front of the text

Abraham Kuruvilla takes these categories and applies them to the exercise of ascertaining the *logos* of a biblical passage.[132] To these categories this

---

[131] Paul Ricoeur, *Hermeneutics and the Human Sciences: Essays on Language, Action and Interpretation*, John B. Thompson, ed., trans. (Cambridge: Cambridge University Press, 1981), 145.

[132] Kuruvilla, *Privilege the Text,* 41.

writer will add the world in the text to the end that the genre, vocabulary, and syntax of Jude will receive some analysis.

THE WORLD BEHIND THE TEXT (HISTORICAL CONTEXT)

Every passage of Scripture has a historical context that must be primary before any application to a contemporary audience can receive application. Every passage of Scripture has a "back then" audience. These real people encountered real problems. Scripture, first addressed to them, must be understood in that light. What did the content and emotional impact of revealed Scripture mean to them? Just why did the Holy Spirit inspire the biblical author to say or write the revelation that was given?

Awareness and consideration of the world behind the text (its historical setting) guide us as we delve into any Scripture passage. There surely must be times when passages not as clearly interpreted by means of the study of vocabulary and syntax receive helpful assistance from the historical dynamics behind such study. This valuable background information gives us impetus to take the content and emotive mode of Scripture and permit it to give maximum influence as we preach a passage of Scripture.

Two considerations result from examining the world behind the text. First, we must consider the setting. What are the circumstances that caused the author of the biblical passage to write? This provides a logical and emotional guide throughout the passage.

Second, we must consider the audience. To whom is the biblical writer speaking? Whomever that might be, the words cannot be adequately understood unless there is a comprehension of their surrounding culture and the worldview that colors their reception.

Deciphering these two considerations does not guarantee total ability to give the full interpretation the exegete and preacher desires. However, such an exercise surely moves toward that goal. Though not a landing strip, such background work provides the exegete and preacher with a helpful launching pad toward full-orbed interpretation.

With these opening insights provided, specific attention to the historical situation (the world behind the text) of the book of Jude is pertinent. As to the historical setting, Jude writes during the closing days of the apostles when apostasy (departure from "the faith once for all delivered to the saints") is on the scene. The predicted departure from the faith already manifests itself. The rolling thunder of dark apostasy makes itself known. A storm of enormous magnitude looms ahead. Jude states the occasion for the letter quite succinctly. False teachers have slipped into the churches through a side door (Jude 4). Pheme Perkins says, "Perhaps those causing trouble were not permanent members of a particular community but wandering teachers or prophets."[133]

Further, as to the historical setting, this writer says in the *Southwestern Journal of Theology*, "It (the purpose) is very easy to discover in the book of Jude since the third verse provides the purpose of the book. Jude is dealing with the subject of apostasy and with apostates."[134]

As to the audience, internal evidence indicates the audience Jude addresses is those who are believers. He says, "To those who are the called . . ." (Jude 1). The preponderance of evidence points toward an audience made up of primarily Jewish Christians who lived in Judaea.[135]

Having done this essential work, there must be further work done. Helm says, "Behind us lie the hills of the ancient text and exegetical work we did on 'them and then.'"[136] The text-driven preacher moves to the second phase of his sermonic work.

---

[133] Pheme Perkins, "First and Second Peter, James and Jude," *Interpretation, a Bible Commentary for Teaching and Preaching* (Louisville: John Knox Press, 1995), 143.

[134] Jerry Vines, "Preaching Through Jude," *The Southwestern Journal of Theology*, Paige Patterson, editor-in-chief, Vol. 58, No.1, Fall 2015), 4.

[135] Herbert W. Bateman, I., "Jude," *Evangelical Exegetical Commentary* (Bellingham: Lexham Press, 2015), 26.

[136] David R. Helm, *I and 2 Peter and Jude* (Wheaton: Crossway, 2008), 87.

THE VITAL ROLE OF *PATHOS*
IN A COMPLETE TEXT-DRIVEN INTERPRETATION OF THE BOOK OF JUDE

THE WORLD IN THE TEXT (GENRE, VOCABULARY, SYNTAX, AND RHETORIC)

The discussion in the previous chapter as to genre gives direction toward our understanding of the same in Jude. Though Jude fits comfortably in the genre designation of letter, further discussion at this juncture informs the exegete of Jude's *logos*. Witherington says, "Jude, like most of the so-called General letters, has suffered from a distinct if not intentional neglect in the Christian world . . . As it fills only one page of text, it hardly deserves to be called a book; it is rather a brief sermon following the conventions of deliberative rhetoric, with an epistolary opening and a doxological conclusion."[137] Witherington adds a rather intriguing reason for Jude's specific place in the New Testament: (It) "is placed where it is in the canon: perhaps a canonical collection of General letters had James first and Jude last, thus framed by sermons from the brothers of Jesus . . ."[138]

The vocabulary, syntactical, and rhetorical analysis of Jude's *logos* will be taken from the writer's *Jude Notebook* submitted to Dr. Terry Wilder in an independent studies format. Not every word in every verse in the entire letter will be given detailed exegesis. Rather, this monograph will focus on primary content in each of the first (vv. 1-4) and the last (vv. 17-25) sections this writer has chosen to identify as the primary preaching paragraphs. The writer takes this approach in order to highlight the importance of understanding the *logos* and especially the *pathos* of those inclusio paragraphs to a more complete exegesis of the body of the letter.

The analysis and importance of *pathos* in passage interpretation still constitutes the primary focus of the monograph. The focus of attention on *logos* interpretation, though general and not exhaustive, further indicates the essential and foremost place of that interpretation in an adequate interpretation of Scripture. Brief notes concerning lexical/syntactical matters and rhetorical analysis will be given for some of the verses in the preaching paragraphs.. Quotations

---

137 Witherington, *Letters and Homilies for Jewish Christians*, 567.
138 Ibid., 571.

from some commentators will be included in the course of those sections. The Greek words will not be used within quotations where the authors who are quoted did not include them.

A recent volume by David J. Clark has a very helpful chapter entitled "A Discourse Analysis of Jude." This represents what might be called "state of the art" in analyzing the syntax of the Greek text in Jude. He gives special attention to "the changes in the person of the verb forms, and (pays) close attention also to lexical recursions and other rhetorical features . . ."[139] His analysis, though helpful, is in more detail than the intentions of the analysis of this writer. But several of his observations based on his analysis are helpful. As to the verbs he says, "It become(s) clear that through the letter there is a movement in the dominant verbs . . ."[140] His chapter relative to Jude also provides an excellent comparison of how various scholars divide the units in the letter.

Jude 1-4

The opening paragraph sets the stage for what follows. The customary greeting is given in verses 1-2. Jude's opening comments are typical of greetings in letters of the New Testament era. Bateman says, "Though expanded Jude's introduction is typical of ancient letters: the sender; the recipients; a greeting."[141] Words indicating Jude's love and appreciation for their status as "called ones" (κλητοῖς) highlights the greeting. They are "loved" (ἠγαπημένοις). The use of the present tense participle carries the sense of God the Father's continual love yesterday, today, and forever for His "called ones."

They are also "kept (τετηρημενοις) by Jesus Christ. Τηρέω conveys the idea of keep watch over, guard someone; or to keep, hold or preserve."[142] The use of the perfect tense participle here carries the sense of continuity. They have

---

139 David J. Clark, *Analyzing and Translating New Testament Discourse* (Dallas: Fontes Press, 2019), n.p.

140 Clark, *Analyzing and Translating,* n.p.

141 Bateman, "Jude," 99.

142 Frederick W. Danker, Walter Bauer, William F. Arndt, and F. Wilbur Gingrich, *Greek-English Lexicon of the New Testament and Other Early Christian Literature*, 3rd ed. (Chicago: University of Chicago Press, 2000), 1002.

been, are, and will continually be kept. Believers are the permanent objects of God's care and protection.

Then follows in verse 2 the customary expression of desire for mercy, peace, and love for the readers. This is the first instance of Jude's fondness of triplets. Dennison says, "What is most noticeable about Jude's style is the symmetry/parallelism of his construction. He is fond of repetition/duplication, even being noted for his penchant for triads . . ."[143] As for the use of the aorist optative translated "desire" (Πληθυνθείη), Davids indicates it "increases the emphatic nature of the blessing . . ."[144]

Also, the use of endearing terms with reference to his readers leads into the use of the most touching reference to them in verse 3.

As a preface to our look at verses 3-4, the words of Watson set them in proper perspective: "Clearly, Jude follows what is called a rhetorical situation, composed of three constituents: the exigence, the audience and the rhetor . . . The exigence is the sudden and troubling infiltration of the church . . . by a doctrinally and ethically divergent group . . ."[145]

In verses 3 and 4, Jude quickly moves to the problem at hand. He prefaces what is to follow by the endearing "Beloved" (Ἀγαπητοί). This verbal adjective is filled with the deepest expression of love for God's people to whom this letter is addressed and urgent warning given. Davids points out that the use of "beloved" marks "the opening of a new section. It will be used similarly in verses 17 and 20 to mark a new section."[146] Far more meaningful than this however, this compassionate, deeply emotional expression of the word serves as a clear indication of the tone Jude sets in these opening verses.

The exigence at hand caused Jude to leave his intended purpose to write about their common salvation and instead exhort them to "contend for the faith that was delivered to the saints once for all." Jude had intended to write to them about the salvation they shared. But a sense of inner compulsion necessitated a

---

143 James T. Dennison, Jr., "The Structure of the Epistle of Jude." *Kerus* 29 (1-May 2014), 1.

144 Peter H. Davids, *2 Peter and Jude: A Handbook on the Greek Text* (Waco: Baylor University Press, 2011), 3.

145 Duane Frederick Watson, *Invention, Arrangement, and Style: Rhetorical Criticism of Jude and II Peter* (Atlanta: Scholars Press, 1988), 29.

146 Davids, *2 Peter and Jude*, 4.

change in subject matter. False apostate teachers were making serious inroads in the churches. So, Jude puts down the harp and takes up the trumpet. Jude hurls a thunderbolt!

The word for "contend" (ἐπαγωνίζομαι) conveys the common use of athletic terminology as metaphors for activities in the Christian life. BDAG gives the meaning, "to exert intense effort on behalf of something."[147] "The faith . . . delivered . . . once for all" is a statement that constitutes that body of truth the apostles transmitted to the church of Christ. Schreiner says, "We have an early recognition here that the touchstone for the Christian faith is the teaching of the apostles and that any deviation from their teaching is unorthodox. cf. Acts 2:42; Jude 17, 20."[148] That body of truth contains the essentials of Christianity: it has to do with the virgin birth of Christ and His blood atonement on the cross. In the New Testament, a clear set of beliefs emerge.

In terms of its structure, Bateman observes that "Jude 4 has five clauses that explain Jude's new purpose: two independent clauses and three very important dependent adj. clauses."[149]

In verse 4, Jude moves specifically to "some people" (τινες ἄνθρωποι), the "ungodly"(ἀσεβεῖς) who "have come in by stealth . . ." (Παρεισεδύησαν). The verb means "to slip in, worm one's way in, join a group unnoticed."[150] Bauckham suggests the word "tends to carry the connotation of secrecy or stealth."[151] They were "designated for this judgment long ago," that is, their condemnation had been written down beforehand. In ancient times, it was customary to post ahead of time the names of defendants who were headed for trial. The judgment of these apostates was scripted long ago. Jude reminds of this for the purpose that believers should not be surprised. Such apostasy happened in the past; it has and will happen again.

---

147 Danker, Bauer, Arndt, and Gingrich, *Greek-English Lexicon of the New Testament*, 356.

148 Thomas R. Schreiner, "1, 2 Peter, Jude," Vol. 37, *The New American Commentary* (Nashville: Broadman and Holman Publishers, 2003), 436.

149 Bateman, "Jude," 139.

150 Davids, *2 Peter and Jude*, 5.

151 Richard J. Bauckham, "Jude, 2 Peter," *Word Biblical Commentary*, Vol. 50 (Waco: Word Books, Publisher, 1983), 35.

They have slipped in for the purpose of "turning the grace of our God into sensuality and denying Jesus Christ . . ." The verb translated "turning" (Μετατιθέντες) is found in the vice lists given in Galatians 5:19 and 1 Peter 4:3. Basically, the word means to change into something else.

The words used to describe the teaching of the apostates are loaded with meaning. "Sensuality" (ἀσέλγειαν) means they have perverted God's saving grace into sexual immorality. BDAG defines it as "Lack of self-constraint which involves one in conduct that violates all bounds of what is socially acceptable, self-abandonment."[152] They also intend to "deny Jesus Christ . . ." which constitutes a denial of Christian doctrine in addition to the subversion of Christian morality. The mention of behavior and doctrine together indicates that one influences the other. What one believes affects how one live; and, conversely, how one lives affects what one believes.

This opening paragraph sets the tone for the body of Jude's letter. Though he minces no words in his initial statement concerning the false teachers or apostates, the readers are addressed in the most loving terms. This must be kept in mind as one works through the body of the letter. To fail to do so, as Gilmore colorfully indicates, would turn Jude into a sick crank instead of a sound critic.

Jude 5-10

The body of Jude's letter generally follows the midrash pattern of moving from text to interpretation of the text. This becomes apparent as Jude moves from past (vv. 5-6, 9) and prophetic aorists (vv. 11, 14) and future tenses (v. 8) to the present tenses in the interpretations that follow. Jude introduces the interpretive passages by οὗτος ("these people") or ουτοι εἰσιν ("these people are").

Jude reminds the readers of passages from the Old Testament that would be already known to them in verses 5-7. The chronological order doesn't guide the references. Rather, there seems to be greater emphasis on the progressive intensity of God's judgment upon the people's unbelief in the wilderness (v. 5), the angels who didn't keep, but abandoned their proper dwelling (v.

---

[152] Danker, Bauer, Arndt, and Gingrich, *Greek-English Lexicon of the New Testament*, 141.

6), and the perversion of Sodom and Gomorrah (v.7). These judgments moved from "destroyed" (ἀπώλεσεν) to "eternal chains in deep darkness" (δεσμοῖς ἀϊδίοις ὑπὸ ζόφον) to "the punishment of eternal fire" (πυρὸς αἰωνίου δίκην ὑπέχουσαι). The placement of these progressively more severe judgements in the text demonstrates powerful rhetorical effect.

The first reference in verse 5 is to Israel in the wilderness. They had been "saved" (σωσας) from slavery in Egypt. This carries the ideal of a physical deliverance from Egypt. The rest of the example makes it obvious that all of them were not "saved" in a spiritual sense. They were "destroyed" (ἀπώλεσεν) due to the fact they "believed not" (μὴ Πιστεύσαντας). Just as today the assumption should not be made that every member of a Christian church is a born-again believer.

The reference to "the angels who did not keep their own position" in verse 6 has been surrounded by a great deal of debate. Clearly, the reference is to the puzzling passage in Genesis 6. Though the text doesn't definitely state that they were angels, "the sons of God," they probably are best interpreted in that manner. Bateman indicates that "the sons of God" are so designated in Jewish tradition. He also refers to Job 1:6; 2:1; and 38:7 referring them to angelic beings.[153] Schreiner emphatically takes the view that Jude "believed angels had sexual relations with women and that God judged the angels for violating their ordained sphere."[154] This writer shares that view.

The connection with the angels who sinned in verse 6 with the sin of Sodom, Gomorrah, and the surrounding towns in verse 7 clearly is made by the use of the comparative conjunction ὡς and the adjective ὅμοιον. The CSB translates these as "likewise." Further, there can be little doubt that their sin manifested itself in "sexual immorality and perversions." "Perversions" translates "ἑτέρας'" which carries the meaning of "flesh of another kind." As the angels sought perverted sexual relations with women, so men in Sodom sought intercourse with other men, contrary to natural sexual activity with woman. The point is that in Sodom the unnatural became natural. Likewise same-sex marriage is rebellion against God's order.

---

153 Bateman, "Jude," 175.
154 Schreiner, "1, 2 Peter, Jude," 45.

Verse 8 begins Jude's application of the Old Testament historical examples to "these people," οὗτοι (the apostate teachers introduced in verse 4). The verse begins with two particles, Μέντοι . . . μέν which point toward the applications Jude will make toward "these people."

Bateman shows that verse 8 structurally has three independent clauses "that reveal the decadent propensity . . . (that) reveals a progressively worsening description . . ."[155] "Relying on their dreams" (ἐνυπνιαζόμενοι) perhaps should be interpreted metaphorically rather than literally. They live in their own dream world of imagination. At Pentecost, reference is made to dreams inspired by the Holy Spirit (Acts 2:17). Here, the reference is undoubtedly to Satan-inspired dreams.

The three statements, "defile their flesh, reject authority, and slander glorious ones" (σάρκα μὲν μιαίνουσιν, κυριότητα δὲ ἀθετοῦσιν, δόξας δὲ βλασφημοῦσιν) reveal the progressively downward depths to which the apostates have descended.

The reference to the narrative of Michael the archangel and his dispute with the devil over Moses's body clearly references an extra-biblical account in 1 Enoch. The preponderance of evidence indicates it came from a book entitled "Assumption of Moses." This does not suggest Jude considers the book to be authoritative Scripture any more than preachers today quoting from events from secular sources so regard them. Though true, that does not mean the preacher considers the entire source as authentic. The intention rather highlights the contrast between the apostate teachers and the archangel Michael. Bateman's comment beautifully expresses the encounter: "Jude presents a verbal progression whereby he paints Michael's entanglement with the devil as an ongoing dispute within a heavenly courtroom where Michael disputes aggressively, like a defense attorney, the prosecuting attorney (the devil)."[156]

In verse 10, Jude turns again to a description of the godless apostates. What they don't understand, they "blaspheme" (βλασφημοῦσιν). What they do understand "by instinct" (φυσικῶς) puts them on the level of "irrational animals" (τὰ ἄλογα ζῷα ἐπίστανται). Their only reasoning is like to that of unreasoning animals. They do understand the power of physical appetites and

---

155 Bateman, "Jude," 196.
156 Ibid., 225.

they plunge right into them. They do understand animal urges and indulge in them. This kind of behavior puts life on the barnyard level. The thrust of the statement is that human beings, in their sexual behavior, shouldn't descend to the level of cats and dogs. And thus, "by these things they are destroyed" (ἐν τούτοις φθείρονται).

Jude 11-16

Some exegetes place Jude 11 with the previous paragraph. Placement in this particular instance does not constitute a crucial decision. This writer chooses to place it with verses 12-16 because the interjection, "Woe" (Οὐαί), that begins the verse leads to the subordinating causal conjunction, "For" (ὅτι), that gives the reasons the "woe" is declared.

As to the "Woe," the interjection occurs numerous times in Old Testament and in New Testament statements of the Lord Jesus. The word occurs significantly in Matthew 23:13-29. Further, the book that follows Jude, Revelation has four occurrences (8:13; 9:12; 11:14; 12:12). "Woe" pronouncements are often used to indicate the severity of the judgement to follow. Just what the use of the word suggests will be discussed in the upcoming chapter on *pathos*.

Continuing in verse 11, Jude makes reference to three Old Testament examples of the kind of behavior of the apostates of his day: "the way of Cain" (τῇ ὁδῷ τοῦ Κάϊν) . . ."Balaam's error" (τῇ πλάνῃ τοῦ Βαλαὰμ) . . ."Korah's rebellion" (τῇ ἀντιλογια τοῦ Κόρε). These three references undoubtedly were familiar to his original audience. They serve as examples of the kind of behavior that always leads to God's judgment.

The three verbs descriptive of the judgment that fell upon them increase in intensity: "gone the way" (ἐπορεύθησαν) . . . "plunged" (ἐξεχύθησαν) and "perished" (ἀπώλοντο). "Gone the way" carries the idea of rushing headlong into a behavior that leads to a disastrous ending. "Plunged" conveys the picture of pouring out, indicating to fully experience something.[157] "Perished," the most intense verb, gives the suggestion of total destruction. Clearly, Jude arranges the examples and uses the vivid language for rhetorical impact.

---

157 Danker, Bauer, Arndt, and Gingrich, *Greek-English Lexicon of the New Testament*, 312.

THE VITAL ROLE OF *PATHOS* IN A COMPLETE TEXT-DRIVEN INTERPRETATION OF THE BOOK OF JUDE

There is a noticeable progression of thought from the nouns that are used ("way . . . error . . . rebellion . . .") and the verbs ("gone . . . plunged . . . perished . . ."). Rhetorical impact cannot be missed by this progression.

From this opening pronouncement of "woe" on these three kinds of behavior, Jude turns to a series of illustrations to describe "these people." Six metaphors in verses 12-13 vividly create the mental images Jude intends. Watson points out that these figures demonstrate the use of enargia, which rhetorically may be used effectively to help people see what one is saying.[158] Bateman says "this accumulation of metaphors refers to apostate Christians who are unregenerate and spiritually isolated from Jesus . . . this compound collection of metaphors . . . express a single concept . . ."[159]

First, they are "dangerous reefs at your love feasts . . ." (Σπιλάδες) follows the preferred reading of this text. The reference is to "a rocky hazard hidden by waves, a rock washed by the sea, a hidden reef."[160]

Second, they are "shepherds who only feed themselves" (Ποιμαίνοντες), that is, self-centered with no intention to feed the members of God's flock.

Third, they are "waterless clouds carried along by winds" (νεφέλαι ἄνυδροι ὑπὸ ἀνέμων παραφερόμεναι). They promise but do not deliver. Just as a farmer whose crops are burning up because of the desperate need of water has his hopes dashed. Seeing a cloud, he anticipates rain. The cloud comes and goes, but no rain. The farmer is left with severe disappointment. So false teachers promise but cannot produce the results suggested by their promises. One thinks about the promises of plenty promised by the prosperity preachers.

Four, they are "trees in late autumn—fruitless, twice dead and uprooted" (δένδρα φθινοπωρινὰ ἄκαρπα δὶς ἀποθανόντα ἐκριζωθέντα) which graphically portrays the utter fruitlessness of apostate teaching. Spiritual fruit is proof of spiritual life (see Matt 7:16). Apostate teaching bears no such fruit. "Twice dead" suggests a first spiritual death and also a second death in the lake

---

[158] Watson, *Invention, Arrangement, and Style,* 61.

[159] Bateman, "Jude," 284.

[160] Danker, Bauer, Arndt, and Gingrich, *Greek-English Lexicon of the New Testament,* 938.

of fire. "Uprooted" metaphorically pictures a life with no stability. They are fruitless because they are rootless.

Five, they are "wild waves of the sea, foaming up their shameful deeds" (κύματα ἄγρια θαλάσσης ἐπαφρίζοντα τὰς ἑαυτῶν αἰσχύνας). Literally, the word ἐπαφρίζοντα means "to cause to splash up like froth, cause to foam."[161] Jude enables the audience to see the waves churning and the filthy foam gathering on the seashore. Vividly, he portrays the slime and corruption the apostates' teaching produces.

Six, they are "wandering stars for whom the blackness is reserved forever" (ἀστέρες πλανῆται, οἷς ὁ ζόφος τοῦ σκότους εἰς αἰῶνα τετήρηται). Again, Jude vividly portrays the utter hopelessness of those who are apostate in their teaching and lifestyle, as are all who follow their teaching.

From these stirring illustrations, Jude moves in verse 14 to a quotation from 1 Enoch 1:9. Undoubtedly, Jude's original audience could be expected to be familiar with it. Such a quotation doesn't indicate that Jude regarded it as divinely inspired. Schreiner explains it quite well: "It is better to conclude that Jude quoted the pseudepigraphical 'I Enoch' and that he also believed that the portion he quoted represented God's truth . . . We do not need to conclude, however, that the entire book is part of the canon of Scripture."[162] As the writer mentioned previously, this would be similar to preachers today quoting from secular sources. Such references would not be construed to suggest endorsement of the totality of such sources.

The repetition of the word "ungodly" (ἀσεβεῖς) in verse 15 is significant. The repetition occurs in different parts of speech—noun, verb, and adverb. Such repetition underscores the severity of the judgement that awaits the apostates at the coming of Christ. Judgment is not only a present reality; even more severe judgment upon "the ungodly" is definitely to come.

This paragraph of Jude concludes in verse 16 with another description of "these people." They are "discontented grumblers" (γογγυσταί, μεμψίμοιροι). "Γογγυσταί" is an example of onomatopoeia, a word that gives its meaning by its pronunciation. BDAG says that is an "utterance made in a low tone of

---

161 Danker, Bauer, Arndt, and Gingrich, *Greek-English Lexicon of the New Testament*, 360.

162 Schreiner, "1, 2 Peter, Jude," 469.

voice, behind-the-scenes talk."¹⁶³ They live "according to their desires" (κατὰ τὰς ἐπιθυμίας αὐτῶν πορευόμενοι). They are totally self-entered.

Finally, "their mouths utter arrogant words . . . flattering . . . for their own advantage" (τὸ στόμα αὐτῶν λαλεῖ ὑπέρογκα, θαυμάζοντες πρόσωπα ὠφελείας χάριν). The picture is of speech that is intended to gain an advantage with people.

Jude 17-25

The use of the vocative "remember" (μνήσθητε) provides a helpful structural signal that there is a transition. This is the first use of the imperative in Jude. The verbal adjective "dear friends"(ἀγαπητοί), used here and also in verse 20 ties the closing paragraph to the opening one (v. 3). Thus, completing the inclusio, which provides the helpful envelope to the body of the letter. Also, note that the emphasis goes from "these" to "you." In the last paragraph Jude turns to his audience with a series of admonitions that will keep them from falling prey to the apostate teachers.

Jude references the predictions of the apostles of the Lord Jesus Christ. His use of "remember" (μνήσθητε) carries more than the idea of mental recall. The implication is that Jude intends his audience to make those words a matter of the heart that will have positive consequences regarding the way they live their lives.

Verse 18 tells them what they had been told previously. In the last days, there would indeed be "scoffers living according to their own ungodly desires" (ἐμπαῖκται κατὰ τὰς ἑαυτῶν ἐπιθυμίας πορευόμενοι τῶν ἀσεβειῶν). All of this the apostles had predicted: Paul (Acts 20:29-30); Peter (2 Pet 2:1-3). And, of course, the Lord Jesus Himself (Matt 24:4-5, 11, 24).

Verse 19 gives Jude's further description of "these people" (Οὗτοί) in another triad. They "create divisions and are worldly, not having the Spirit" (οἱ οἱ ἀποδιορίζοντες, ψυχικοί, Πνεῦμα μὴ ἔχοντες, ψυχικοί, Πνεῦμα μὴ ἔχοντες). The word translated "create divisions" (οἱ ἀποδιορίζοντες) is an hapax legomenon, occurring only here in the New Testament. Schreiner suggests that this

---

163 Danker, Bauer, Arndt, and Gingrich, *Greek-English Lexicon of the New Testament*, 204.

particular word "could mean that the intruders made distinctions between people. Some they classified as spiritual and some unspiritual."[164] Such dividers unfortunately are found in the church today. They form spiritually elite groups that divide the church between those who are "in the know" and the rest of the congregation. And, if you don't "go along," you are a troublemaker.

"Worldly" (ψυχικοί) refers to the fact that they are governed by their sensuous nature. So "spiritual" are these "elites" that the normal rules and standards do not apply to them.

The final description "not having the Spirit" (Πνεῦμα μὴ ἔχοντες) gives the most severe pronouncement of all. Jude makes it abundantly clear that the apostate teachers are unsaved.

In verse 20, Jude moves to the specific admonitions he has for believers who are to maintain their walk with the Lord and withstand the dangers and avoid the pitfalls of the apostates' false teaching and the lifestyle it produces. Verses 20-21 are interesting grammatically. The repetition of "dear friends" ("beloved") indicates another transition in the flow of thought.

The central exhortation is seen in verse 22. "Keep yourselves in the love of God" (ἑαυτοὺς ἐν ἀγάπῃ Θεοῦ τηρήσατε) has the second use of the imperative (τηρήσατε) in Jude's letter. The verb τηρέω might be called the melodic line of Jude. Helm says, "Each book has a melodic line, an essence that informs what the book is about . . . at the beginning and the end of the book, A single sound began to emerge: being kept . . ."[165] Note the contrast: There is a keeping God does (see v. 1) and there is a keeping believers do. God's is the keeping of salvation; that of the believer is the keeping of sanctification. Though God loves them continually and He powerfully keeps them, they must keep themselves in the atmosphere of His love. The sun is shining, but we may take ourselves out of the warmth of that sun.

Around this aorist active imperative, Jude wraps three present participles that show how believers may keep themselves in the love of God. Though present tense participles, their close relationship to the central imperative gives them the weight of imperatives as well.

---

164 Schreiner, "1, 2 Peter, Jude," 479.
165 Helm, *1 and 2 Peter and Jude*, 47-49.

First, they are to build themselves up: "as you build yourselves up in your most holy faith"(ἐποικοδομοῦντες ἑαυτοὺς τῇ ἁγιωτάτῃ ὑμῶν πίστει). The figure is from architecture. As a house is built upon a foundation, so the Christian life is to be built upon the foundational experience of a saving experience with Jesus (1 Cor 3:11). This is accomplished as the believer builds himself up through the study of God's Word (Acts 20:32).

Second, they keep themselves in God's love by "praying in the Holy Spirit" (ἐν Πνεύματι Ἁγίῳ προσευχόμενοι). There is no suggestion that a heavenly language is to be articulated. The preposition "ἐν" is locative of sphere. All true prayer is in the sphere of the Holy Spirit, motivated and empowered by Him.

The third present participle is in verse 21, "waiting expectantly for the mercy of our Lord Jesus Christ for eternal life" (προσδεχόμενοι τὸ ἔλεος τοῦ Κυρίου ἡμῶν Ἰησοῦ Χριστοῦ εἰς ζωὴν αἰώνιον). BDAG says that προσδεχόμενοι means "to look forward to the fulfillment of our expectation (Titus 2:13), await (the realization of) (Acts 24:15)."[166] Believers should be characterized by intense, expectant waiting for the Lord's return.

"Building . . . praying . . . waiting" are the three activities that will keep believers then and now in God's love and keep them from falling prey to the apostates' false teaching.

Verses 22-23 turn the attention to the responsibility of believers, not only to maintain their own relationship with God, but to bear witness to others. The structure of this section is not easy to determine. Are there two or three groups to whom believers must witness? Schreiner says, "Some witnesses divide the text into two clauses while other witnesses divide it into three . . . Certainly on whether the text should be divided into two or three clauses cannot be attained . . ."[167]

The relative pronoun "οὖσ" occurs three times. This writer tends to follow the structure of the Christian Standard Bible. Jude gives three groups to whom believers must bear witness. First, "Have mercy on those who waver" (οὓς μὲν ἐλεᾶτε διακρινομένουσ). The CSB translation of διακρινομένους,

---

166 Danker, Bauer, Arndt, and Gingrich, *Greek-English Lexicon of the New Testament*, 877.

167 Schreiner, "1, 2 Peter, Jude," 486.

"those who waver," is much preferred over the King James translation, "making a difference." The idea is probably that there are those who are wavering because of the insidious teaching of the apostates.

Second, they are to "save others by snatching them from the fire" (οὓς δὲ σῴζετε ἐκ πυρὸς ἁρπάζοντες). These words call to mind the statement in Zechariah 3:2 about being "snatched from the fire." Some are near death and eternal fire in hell. These are to be brought to Christ with a sense of urgency.

Third, there are those whose lives are so filled with the filth of sin that they must be witnessed to "with fear, hating even the garment defiled by the flesh" (ἐν φόβῳ, μισοῦντες καὶ τὸν ἀπὸ τῆς σαρκὸς ἐσπιλωμένον χιτῶνα). Could this be a direct reference to the apostates whose lives would be aptly described by such language?

The χιτῶνα was an inner garment worn next to the flesh, corresponding to our undergarments. "Defiled" (ἐσπιλωμένον) directly refers to a defilement caused by human excrement. Schreiner says, "Such a picture shocks the readers with how polluting and corrupting sin is . . ."[168] So corrupt is their lifestyle that the Christian witness is to be very cautious he/she doesn't become defiled by the contact. The witness must exercise extreme care in this kind of witnessing endeavor.

Jude closes his book with a doxological flourish. Such oratorical flourish fits well with the sermonic nature of his book. Verses 24-25 may very well be considered the most beautiful of all the doxologies in the New Testament.

Verse 24 begins the doxology "Now to him who is able to protect you from stumbling . . ." (Τῷ δὲ δυναμένῳ φυλάξαι ὑμᾶς ἀπταίστους). "Now to Him who is able" (Τῷ δὲ δυναμένῳ). The New Testament is replete with references to the ability of God. God indeed is omnipotent!

A different word for keeping is used here (φυλάξαι). "Stumbling" (ἀπταίστους) does not suggest losing salvation. Rather, the picture is taken from the stumbling of a horse in battle. The believer can be protected even from the stumbling they might indeed experience as they live the Christian life.

"And to make you stand in the presence of his glory, without blemish and great joy" (καὶ στῆσαι κατενώπιον τῆς δόξης αὐτοῦ ἀμώμους ἐν ἀγαλλιάσει) beautifully expresses the glorious day that awaits believers when

---

168 Schreiner, "1, 2 Peter, Jude," 489.

they stand at last in the presence of their Lord, with no blemish and with exulting joy. What a day that will be! Schreiner says about "without blemish" that the term "is used of Old Testament sacrifices . . . of Jesus as a perfect sacrifice . . . and of believers on the day of judgement" (Eph 1:4; 5:27; Col 1:22).[169]

Jude could not be more profound than what we find in verse 25 in his final word of praise to "God our Savior, through Jesus Christ our Lord" (μόνῳ Θεῷ Σωτῆρι ἡμῶν διὰ Ἰησοῦ Χριστοῦ τοῦ Κυρίου ἡμῶν). Then comes the fourfold doxological anthem: "glory, majesty, power, and authority . . ." (δόξα μεγαλωσύνη κράτος καὶ ἐξουσία). Davids says the four words are "generally understood as a series of honor words."[170] Bateman says about this conclusion that believers "are lifted from earth to the heavenly realms, where God resides enthroned with ultimate power and authority as the majestic ruler over all His created order."[171]

And, then the duration of the praise: "before all time, now and forever. Amen" (παντὸς τοῦ αἰῶνος καὶ νῦν καὶ εἰς πάντας τοὺς αἰῶνας· ἀμήν). This ending is better and more complete than the King James rendering "both now and forever." This ascribes to all past time, present time, and future time everything Jude has said about God the Father and Jesus Christ the Son.

The writer intends by this exegesis of the text of Jude to give a taste of the importance of *logos* analysis of the words Jude uses, their structural and syntactical relationships, and primary importance in text-driven interpretation. As this writer states in several places in the monograph, content is the primary and first consideration. However, toward the argument of this monograph, the writer argues that to interpret scriptural texts as to their content (*logos*) alone does not give the fullest, most complete interpretation possible.

David Helm gives helpful understanding relative to the insufficiency of merely exegeting passage content. He says, "Intellectual preaching occurs when you make the first audience your final concern . . ."[172] He correctly indicates that if you stop with the mere textual content analysis, the resulting

---

169 Schreiner, "1, 2 Peter, Jude," 491.
170 Davids, *2 Peter and Jude*, 40.
171 Bateman, "Jude," 439.
172 Helm, *1 and 2 Peter and Jude*, 57.

sermons are not adequate. He continues, "It's what happens when you take a profoundly relevant text and render it irrelevant by writing sermons that read like an academic commentary. You do the work of exegesis but stop. You end up with boring, ineffective, well-footnoted speeches . . . (preachers make the mistake "that the sermon is . . . a storage container for housing everything they learned about the text that week)."[173] To this view the writer would add—the work of exegesis itself is not complete with mere content interpretation. The work of *pathos* analysis must also be done to give a complete, well-orbed interpretation of Scripture. *Logos* interpretation alone leaves the content of Scripture flat on the pages. The addition of *pathos* interpretation makes Scripture come alive on the pages.

THE WORLD IN FRONT OF THE TEXT (APPLICATION TO CONTEMPORARY CULTURE)

A consideration of the world in front of the text must be clarified. This has to do with the intention of the biblical author as to the meaning of what he writes for those who will read it in the future. E. D. Hirsch indicates that Bible authors had trans-historical intentions that guided the use of their words with future applications in mind.[174] This especially deserves attention for those who exegete and proclaim Scripture for purposes of application and life change on the part of those who receive the message.

    The goal of preaching Bible texts must not be to give a full explanation of what the texts meant only to those who resided in the world behind the text. On an occasion, the writer heard a very gifted, well-trained, godly pastor preach on Psalm 23. The pastor gave tremendous background information about shepherds and sheep. When the message concluded, this writer left the service with the question, So what?

---

    173   Helm, *1 and 2 Peter and Jude*, 58.
    174   E. D. Hirsch, "Transhistorical Intentions and the Persistence of Allegory," *New Literary History* 25 (1994): 549-67.

THE VITAL ROLE OF *PATHOS* IN A COMPLETE TEXT-DRIVEN INTERPRETATION OF THE BOOK OF JUDE

On another occasion, the writer heard a favorite radio preacher speak on the magi who came to see the newborn king. The country from which they came, the camels upon which they rode, and the technicalities of their journey extended to several days of broadcasting. Again, when the messages were completed, the writer responded with the question, So what?

To remain in the Bible world and not bring textual meaning into the contemporary world for purposes of application and life change misses the ultimate goal of text-driven preaching. The biblical exegete must not content himself with giving the history and happenings of the past and the technical aspects of textual study. The further step must be taken to move to meaningful applications based on the timeless truths found in the texts of Scripture.

As shall become apparent in further chapters, ascertaining textual *pathos* (emotional mode) greatly assists this bringing of Scripture meaning into the world in front of the text. Just as there are timeless truths as to the *logos* of Scripture (its content meaning), there are timeless emotions apparent in the texts that may be interpreted as well. Joy is a common emotion experienced by people in any age. The experience of grief knows no time restrictions. The whole range of human emotions experienced by the first readers (or hearers) of Scripture may be experienced by those who hear Scripture *pathos* interpreted today.

The target of enabling those who listen to Scripture proclamation today does not end itself in helping people today just feel certain emotions in and of themselves. Rather, there must be a transfer of the emotions found in a Scripture passage through a preacher to those who live in the world beyond the text.

When done correctly, the application of emotional modes found in biblical texts will not take away from their *logos*, but will enhance them by the accompanying emotions thus created then and now. Wrapped around the timeless truths of Scripture, *logos* is the emotions that apply, regardless of when and who constitutes the audience in the world beyond the text. The preacher in the contemporary world should be able to convey this emotional wrapping and apply it to the world today. Therefore, to accurately interpret periscopes of Scripture, the *pathos* must be a partner of the *logos* found therein. To fail to find the *pathos* of the world in the text and in the world before it will cripple any attempt to adequately apply Scripture to our world beyond the text.

This purpose to look to the world beyond the text has application to our consideration of the book of Jude as an example of the necessity of *pathos* interpretation. Jude not only intends to warn his listeners and readers about the dangers of apostates and their apostasy. His warnings surely thrust themselves forward to apply to believers of every successive age. Such biblical application safeguards from allowing the culture to determine the beliefs of God's people. We must not conform our preaching to whatever may be the opinions of the day. Spurgeon said, "We shall not adjust our Bible to the age; but . . . we shall adjust the age to the Bible."[175]

---

175 R. Bruce Bickel, *Light and Heat: The Puritan View of the Pulpit* (Morgan, PA: Soli Deo Gloria Publications, 1999), 69-70.

Chapter Four

Exegetical Summary of Jude's *Pathos*

Chapter four brings this monograph closer to its main thesis. The writer moves forward with the clear recognition that Scripture *logos* is the first and most essential ingredient in any interpretation of a pericope of God's Word. For this reason, the previous chapter gives attention to that vital aspect of Bible interpretation.

Now, the writer drills into the preaching paragraphs of the book of Jude as to the emotional mode that wraps around this *logos* content. There will be no ironclad enumerating of the various emotions found layered around the paragraphs. Such would fail to recognize that all interpreters will identify and describe passage *pathos* as their insights, backgrounds, and God-given abilities enabling them.

Special attention will be given to the opening (vv. 1-4) and closing (vv. 17-25) paragraphs and the tender, compassionate emotions found in each. This moves the monograph forward by showing these envelope paragraphs form an inclusio for the book of Jude. Failure to take these paragraphs into consideration in the interpretation of Jude leads to a failure to understand and correctly set forth the overall message of the book. This failure leads to missing the positive, encouraging thrust of the letter. Further, such places the author, Jude, in an unfavorable light, thus skewing the true picture of his compassionate concern.

As John Gilmore points out, "Jude didn't spare exposing those who crept into the church but were unable to adhere to the apostolic given (v.4) . . ." He continues: "Jude was not blasting his immediate audience but those once removed. Notice the affection Jude expressed in the way he addressed his readers, 'dear friends'(three times—vv. 3, 17, 20). The final words of Jude (vv. 18-25) constitute the main point of the letter. They are upbeat and positive. A superficial scanning of the book of Jude leads to the opinion that Jude was nasty."[176] Gilmore further says, "Initially Jude comes across as a screaming eagle, but in his deepest heart he was a lonesome, peace-loving, peace-pursuing dove. He was grieved that evil had abounded."[177] Edwards concurs: "Jude begins and ends on a positive note and so the letter should not be appraised as a negative tract but as a positive encouragement for the readers."[178]

In a picturesque manner, Gilmore describes Jude's intention: "Jude was not a stone thrower, but a brick layer . . . his book shows the artistry of a person accustomed to speaking. Jude was a traveling speaker, a fact mentioned in 1 Corinthians 9:5. His book shows a well-honed speaking style. He was candid, concise, and colorful . . . at his command was a large stock of Greek words that had a stately and sonorous effect.is rich vocabulary and his artistic rhetoric makes (sic) his book a model of excellent writing."[179]

Leading into this writer's analysis of passage *pathos* for the preaching paragraphs, several general statements need to be made. First, general rhetorical features call for attention. Jude writes in typical first-century letter writing fashion. As noted by Bateman, three component parts to his letter cannot be missed: the opening address and greeting, the body of the letter, and the closing salutation.[180]

Witherington's groundbreaking work as to the rhetorical features of Scripture provides helpful information regarding Jude. He says, "Our author's rhetorical strategy is rather simple (by) . . . midrashic handling of scriptural texts . . . and artificial (creation of colorful similes) proofs he will show that these false ones are like other such false persons who had disastrous effects

---

176 Gilmore, *Sick Crack or Sound Crick?*, 15.
177 Ibid., 16.
178 Jeffrey L. Edwards, "The Literary Structure of Jude and How It Affects the Interpretation of 'the Faith' in Jude 3," Research Paper, Baptist Bible Seminary, Clarks Summit, April 2012, 9.
179 Gilmore, *Sick Crack or Sound Crick?*, 24.
180 Bateman, "Jude," 11.

on the people of God . . . We can see Jude as a deliberative discourse, with the polemical volume turned up in places, from start to finish."[181]

Second, a number of rhetorical devices present themselves as fruitful resources of understanding for the interpreter and reader. Clearly, Jude received training in the use of rhetoric as a means of persuasion. Gilmore says Jude's book "shows the artistry of a person accustomed to speaking . . . his book shows a well-honed speaking style. He was candid, concise, and colorful."[182] More than that, his book is so filled with words rich in *pathos* and so evident in rhetorical artistry that the reader cannot miss the effect intended.

This does not diminish in any way the recognition that the ultimate persuader is the Holy Spirit, who inspired Jude to write. But Edwards states the obvious: "Just as the expert speaker was able to communicate stylistic features such as rhythm, alliteration, precision, accent and brevity . . . (so Jude) was careful to exploit every possible device for maximum effect with his audience."[183] This does not mean, however, that Jude is restricted to them as the only means of persuasion. Jude, as all writers of Scripture, has the ultimate communication advantage—the inspiration and illumination of the Holy Spirit.

Third, a careful analysis of Jude's content demonstrates that he makes use of *pathos* with the intention of persuasion. "As one reads Jude there are several obvious attempts by Jude to stir the hearts and minds of his audience which he does by using highly charged words to describe the work of the enemy."[184]

The rhetorical and spiritual goal of negative and positive behaviors of the readers receives impetus by Jude's intentional use of those devices. Again, Edwards says, "(Jude's) goal was to convince people to avoid the direction that leads to judgment and to choose the direction that leads to life. He did this by appealing to his audience through words which are packed with emotion and logic."[185]

Gilmore makes the perceptive observation that "Jude was not a stone thrower, but a brick layer . . . he did not incoherently rave."[186]

---

181 Witherington, *Letters and Homilies for Jewish Christians*, 597.
182 Gilmore, *Sick Crack or Sound Crick?*, 24.
183 Ibid., 15.
184 Ibid., 30.
185 Ibid., 32.
186 Ibid., 24.

Jude 1-4

The introductory verses of Jude provide fertile soil for rhetorical analysis in general as well as *pathos* analysis in particular. They provide much insight into *ethos* as well as *logos* and *pathos*. Verse 1 opens the letter with a clear statement of Jude as the author and his self description as "a servant of Jesus Christ and a brother of James" (CSB). The clear relationship with the respected James as one of his brothers serves to give immediate credibility to Jude. His relationship with Jesus Christ as "a servant" rather than "a brother" establishes *ethos* humility. Because he has no intention to assert himself beyond servanthood status, surely this gives the initial readers respect for Jude and an inclination to hear him with positive inclinations. The letter begins with a personal, warm statement of authorship. Surely the original readers would have been inclined to respond with the same kind warmth and positive response.

Verse 1 continues with a description of Jude's original readers, and by extension, all believers who would read in the future. "To those who are the called, loved by God the Father and kept for Jesus Christ." These words are filled with gratitude, appreciation, and a strong sense of Christian identification with them. The use of the present tense participle ("loved") to describe those who are identified by the verbal adjective as "the called" in an introductory manner creates the emotion of gratitude for the reality that God's called people are not just one time but are continually loved by the heavenly Father.

The use of the perfect participle ("kept") conveys the meaning that God's people have been kept, are right now and will be kept safe continually. The use of the preposition "for" before "Jesus Christ" surely catches the spirit of what Jude is saying. Bauckham adds, "This phrase has an eschatological sense: Christians are kept safe by God for the Parousia of Jesus Christ when they will enter into their final salvation in his kingdom."[187]

The sense of appreciation and gratitude Jude thus expresses surely intends to create the same emotions on the part of the readers of his letter. The opening statement wraps the readers in the warm blanket of Christian identity, fellowship, love, and assurance. The thunder and lightening of judgment approaching is prefaced by Jude's pastoral concern evidenced in the opening pericope.

---

187 Bauckham, "Jude, 2 Peter," 26.

Jude's tendency to make use of triads emerges at the outset of his letter. His readers are "called . . . loved and kept." This first of many triads should give some insight into the reality that Jude's fondness for symmetry and parallelism in syntactical construction gives emotional responses of pleasantness and ease of reading. (Note: James Dennison's excellent article, "The Structure of the Epistle of Jude," explores this in more depth.)

Verse 2 gives the normal greeting found in letters of that time and in the letters of Scripture. The greeting contains another triplet in Jude. The use of the optative verb, Πληθυνθείη, conveys the wish or desire that these three spiritual blessings become realities in the lives of the readers. Such an expression of good will and desire for blessings surely calls forth positive emotions because it demonstrates the great love and respect Jude has for them.

Verse 3 continues expressions of love on Jude's part. This word is used in verses 17 and 20 to mark a transition to a new section in the letter. Ἀγαπητοί is translated "dear friends" in the CSB. This writer prefers to translate the more commonly used translation "beloved" (see KJV, NKJV, ESB, NASB). This seems to translate the verbal adjective so as to convey the warm *pathos* obviously intended.

Jude shares with the readers his intention to write about "the salvation we share." Such a discussion surely would have been filled with deep expressions of emotion. But, moving in a more necessary direction, given the disturbing developments, Jude introduces words that suggest numerous emotions: "appealing"—a sense of plea and urging; "to contend for . . ."—emotions surrounding battle, a formidable enemy, and things worth fighting for are suggested by these emotion-laden words. "The faith that was delivered to the saints once for all." The CSB helpfully gives the specific meaning indicated by the definite article with "faith" and the sense of the adverb, which in context carries the idea of "once for all." Such language points to the basic teaching of the apostles which serves as the corpus of Christian doctrine from which any deviation leads to heresy. The completeness and finality of the Christian revelation surely carry the emotional impact of appreciation, value, and the determination to maintain are communicated in the wording.

Verse 4 goes directly to the pressing problem about which Jude must warn. Such an abrupt transition to "some people . . . have come in by stealth .

. . ." (in the CSB, the writer prefers "certain men") must be construed to be Jude's intention to signal extreme urgency. These false teachers "(coming) in by stealth" surely give cause for alarm as the word is used in other contexts of an alligator slipping into the water to pursue prey.

The words that follow—"ungodly, turning the grace of our God into sensuality and denying Jesus Christ . . ." are filled with vividness that also flood the mind with a profusion of emotional concern. Consider the word translated "sensuality" (ἀσέλγειαν). BDAG defines it as a "lack of self-constraint which involves one in conduct that violates all bounds of what is socially acceptable, self-abandonment."[188] The word surely calls forth pictures of total abandonment to fleshly lusts and over-the-top immoral living.

In summary, the opening paragraph moves the reader from emotions of love, joy, peace, appreciation, etc. to emotions of concern, alarm, and apprehension. Failure to recognize this contrasting *pathos* renders the preaching passage weak and lacking in the intended fervor. Further, to fail to see that Jude prefaces his more severe and harsh statements in the two central paragraphs of his letter with warm love and concern for his readers tends to make Jude just a diatribist. To correctly interpret his introductory remarks enables us to view Jude as what he surely shows himself to be—a man with genuine pastoral concerns for the welfare of endangered believers.

Jude 5-10

Though beyond the purview of this monograph, the stylistic features that come into play in this section and the next (vv. 11-16) may have some suggestions concerning the *pathos* created by their variation. Bauckham notes that the sections use past verb tenses (vv. 5-6, 9), prophetic aorists (vv. 11, 14), and future tenses (v. 8) in the presentation of three historical examples to prove his assertion in verse 4.[189] These variations serve to make the examples more vivid and in such manner heighten the emotional response of the readers.

---

188 Danker, Bauer, Arndt, and Gingrich, *Greek-English Lexicon of the New Testament*, 141.

189 Bauckham, "Jude, 2 Peter," 4.

There unfolds in this section a recognizable pattern. Jude refers to Scripture; then offers interpretation. Witherington says, "Jude has abundant use of Scripture followed by interpretation and application in a midrash pesher (comes from a Hebrew word meaning interpretation) fashion . . ."[190] Jude provides a good example for the would-be text-driven preacher!

Now Jude begins to demonstrate that what he says about the false teachers in verse 4 corresponds to the actual circumstances about which he warns. He begins in verse 5 with "Now I want to remind you . . ." This indicates the readers already know about the historical facts Jude will cite as historical illustrations to point to the "certain men" who endanger their faith. Bateman says, "All these things" is a "cataphoric (a word in a text that refers to another word later in the text). Thus, it refers to three historical events."[191] These events serve as proof that "certain men . . . were designated for this judgment long ago" (v. 4).

Jude will use these three historical events to make his case. The first one in verse 5 is the deliverance of the chosen people out of Egypt. Looking back on the Exodus event, Jude surely elicited the emotions of gratitude and appreciation by this mention. The two contrasting words "saved . . . destroyed . . ." are informative. Whether the verb form translated "destroyed" refers either to the more common meaning of physical death or eternal destruction, as used in Matthew 10:28, an interpretation that the emotion of alarm is intended carries weight. Hebrew Scripture vividly narrates these contrasting scenes. Emotions of exhilaration for deliverance from Egypt and sadness for the unbelief of some that led to destruction prominently contrast with one another.

The placement of "destroyed" (ἀπώλεσεν) last in the verse carries *pathos* significance. Waiting until the end to place the word indicates an intention to heighten the rhetorical effect and increase the emotions so intended by the use of the word.

Verse 6 gives the second historical example Jude cites to make definite his case that judgment lies ahead for those mentioned in verse 4. Jude refers to "the angels who did not keep their own position but abandoned their proper dwelling . . ." There is considerable debate and difference of opinion as to just

---

190 Witherington, *Letters and Homilies for Jewish Christians*, 573.
191 Bateman, "Jude," 168.

what this reference means. Again, the writer does not intend to enter in to this discussion. Rather, the emotive dynamics of this debatable reference call attention in this monograph.

An interesting contrast in *pathos* is indicated by Jude's repetition of τηρέω found in verse 1 in reference to the safekeeping of believers for the return of Christ. To use the same verb in reference to the rebellion of angels as to their failure to "keep their own position" suggests an emotive change from joy to sorrow, from anticipation to dread, and from deliverance to defeat. Then, note a further shift in the use of the word: "He (God) has kept . . ." One cannot miss the change in *pathos*. The emotive tone shifts to recognition of God's justice in reserving the fallen angels to a final judgment.

"Eternal chains in deep darkness" conveys emotions of solemnity and finality. "For the judgment on that great day" should produce a sense of awe and gratitude at the final resolution of injustice.

The third historical example begins in verse 7. The example of God's judgment on Sodom and Gomorrah used here by Jude has also been the subject of quite a bit of various interpretation and scholarly debate. This monograph does not enter into the precise meaning of the Sodom and Gomorrah reference. Rather, the *pathos* suggested by several words should be evaluated. As to "sexual immorality and perversions," displeasure and offense flow from the words.

This writer prefers the more literal "went after flesh of another kind" over "perversions." Perhaps this reflects the writer's belief that the reference is to homosexuality, which is sexual relations between individuals "of another kind," that is, a seeking of relations outside that which God intends. If this is correct, the emotive content is a reactionary and distasteful aversion to such behavior.

The primary focus as to *pathos* in this historical example centers on the judgment suffered as a result of Sodom and Gomorrah's sin. "The punishment of eternal fire" again creates negative emotions that are filled with solemnity, horror, and a sense of finality.

Notice should be taken that Jude lists the three historical examples out of their chronological order as found in the Old Testament. There seems to be a rhetorical purpose in this. The judgment of God upon Sodom & Gomorrah contains more severity than the other two. Further, Sodom & Gomorrah clearly parallel the sexual sin of the "dreamers, who defile the flesh" in verse eight.

Having cited the three historical examples to prove his case, Jude turns again in verse 8 to those he calls "these people" (the writer prefers "these men"). The section begins with the particles Μέντοι, an adversative-coordinating conjunction meaning, "nevertheless," and μέν, an alternating particle, meaning "on the one hand." This writer translates them, "But likewise also . . ." The words point forward to the exposition of Jude relative to "these men" introduced in verse 4 and compared to in the three historical examples of verses 5-7. The transition or turning back to "these men" serves as an emotive pause and anticipatory mood as to the application of the historical examples.

One detects sarcasm and disdain in Jude's "relying on their dreams . . ." The words "defile . . . reject . . . and slander . . ." indicate Jude's intended impact by these strongly emotive words. Such words cannot but help call forth strong *pathos* in the hearts and minds of those who read (or hear) them.

Verse 9 includes Jude's example of Michael the archangel's refusal to blasphemously pronounce judgment upon the devil. "Disputing . . . in an argument about Moses' body." The clash and controversy of those words have their particular *pathos*. "The Lord rebuke you" surely conveys deep conviction that judgment belongs to God alone and not to angels or men.

But, the contrast with the behavior of "certain men" in verse 10 has its intended emotive impact. "These people blaspheme anything they do not understand." One does not have to imagine a great deal to sense the surprise and amazement in the words Jude employs to describe the audacity of the false teachers to whom he refers. "And what they do understand by instinct—like irrational animals—by these things they are destroyed." These words also emote surprise and amazement. And the sense of impending destruction by the word "destroyed" cannot be missed. A different verb is used here than that of verse 5. Here the verb is Φθείρονται, which carries the idea of corruption leading to destruction.

Careful analysis of the *pathos* in this second preaching paragraph yields much fruit for the diligent interpreter. Witherington says, "The rhetorical intent and effect of this colorful language was to create a negative emotional response, to create *pathos*, in this case appealing to one's sense of fear and horror at betrayal and shameful behavior."[192]

Jude 11-16

Verse 11 begins the third preaching paragraph (though some interpreters prefer to include verse 11 with verses 5-10). The opening "woe" (οὐαὶ) is an interjection pointing back to the false teachers to whom Jude refers and pointing forward to the judgment that awaits them. ὅτι, a subordinating causal conjunction, which means "because" or "since," points to the reasons there rests a "woe" upon the false teachers. Watson says, "The traditional woe formula beginning (in) verse 11 is an example of exclamation and is designed to elicit *pathos*. With it, Jude is able to express great emotion precipitated by the severity of the audacity of the sectarians described in verses 8-10 and try to elicit the same emotion from his audience."[193]

For the interpreter of this passage, a consideration of the *pathos* indicated by Jude's use of "woe" provides some assistance. Just what does this "woe" indicate? Does Jude use the word in an uncontrollable, angry, hateful way? A cross reference to the words of Jesus provides some interpretive direction. Jesus used "woe" on several occasions, in particular the well-known "woes" of Matthew 23.

How does the word as used by Jesus assist us here? What kind of emotional tone does His use of the word convey? Does it express an uncontrollable outburst of anger on the part of the Lord? This writer would take a view to the contrary. Rather, an emotion of wounded love corresponds more readily to what Scripture reveals about Jesus. Likewise, Jude's use of the word doesn't have to be one of anger either. An interpretation similar to that made in regard to Jesus seems to fit the overall tone of the letter more correctly. Jude is not angry; he is warning. He has no outburst of uncontrollable hatred; he speaks with compassion and sorrow.

The "woe" introduces three more historical examples, not events, but people, who serve as warnings of certain judgment. Jude's use of a triad again

---

192 Witherington, *Letters and Homilies for Jewish Christians*, 622.
193 Watson, *Invention, Arrangement, and Style*, 58.

serves to emphasize and heighten the sense of *pathos*. The descriptions of Cain, Balaam, and Korah build an intensity of emotion: "the way of Cain . . . Balaam's error for profit . . . Korah's rebellion . . ."

Also, there is an intensity building that creates greater and greater concern by the three verbs used to describe the behavior of Cain, Balaam, and Korah "have gone the way . . . have plunged . . . have perished . . ."

Verses 12-13 contain a series of examples Jude uses to describe the false teachers. Davids points out that the structure in this section is difficult because the denunciation is intense.[194] The Spirit-inspired selection of words of Jude demonstrates rising *pathos*. There are six metaphors found herein. The accumulation of these gives a stirring, chilling picture of apostates, lost and without any relationship to the Savior. In terms of their emotive content, Bateman says, "This compound collection of metaphors may simply be a type of hendiadys (the expression of a single idea by use of several words) where coordinate metaphors express a single concept . . ."[195] Watson says they exhibit "the figure of *enargesis*, that is, a vivid illustration or representation to create mental pictures and invigorate style. *Enargia* is particularly useful in arousing *pathos*."[196] Surely these various rhetorical devices have the pronounced intention to create certain emotional responses. The overwhelming accumulation has the effect of minimizing the *ethos* of the apostates and enhancing their negative *pathos*.

Consider the metaphors in verse 12. "These people are dangerous reefs at your love feasts." Emotions suggested by the danger of hidden rocks that are capable of great harm and a sense of betrayal at the deception involved at the fellowship meal cannot be missed. "They are shepherds who only look after themselves." Disgust at shepherds (spiritual leaders) who care not for the sheep (God's people) permeates this phrase. "They are waterless clouds carried along by winds." A sense of futile expectation disappointed by the unfulfilled promise of refreshing water presents itself in this metaphor. "Trees in late autumn—fruitless, twice dead and uprooted." Disappointed expectation and frustrated desire for fruit serves as a stirring metaphor for the anticipation of spiritual fruit from these false teachers.

---

194 Davids, *2 Peter and Jude*, 19.
195 Bateman, "Jude," 284.
196 Watson, *Invention, Arrangement, and Style*, 61.

Verse 13 continues this metaphorical assault upon the spiritual sensitivities of Jude's audience. "They are wild waves of the sea, foaming up their shameful deeds." The picture of foam heaving upon the shore with its filth and trash vividly portrays the kind of results transpiring from the teaching of apostates. Bauckham almost equals the emotive language of Jude as he says, "They have roared like turbulent seas, and their towering waves have spat out mud and slime (quote from a Qumran hymn)."[197] "Wandering stars for whom the blackness of darkness is reserved forever." Such emotion-laden words build the rhetorical crescendo surely intended by Jude. "Wandering stars" pictures the desperation which results from being left to being without direction or destiny. Such will be the disastrous results of those who are duped by false teachers. "The blackness of darkness forever" could hardly be more moving as to the dark, dark night of the soul so driven by their apostate teaching. At this point in his letter Jude has marshalled a host of rhetorical pictures to create tremendous negative *pathos* as it relates to false teachers, what they teach, and the damaging, damning results that follow.

Verses 14-15 contain Jude's reference to the statements recorded in 1 Enoch 1:9. This monograph does not enter into the various considerations about Jude's use of extra-biblical material. Suffice it to say that Jude's quotation from 1 Enoch does not suggest that the entire book is God's truth and should be included in the canon of Scripture. Rather, the intention is to comment upon the *pathos* contained in the quotation. The first obvious observation is the repetition of the word "ungodly." The word is repeated four times in verse 15. The word is first a noun (two times), then a verb, and lastly an adverb. Like the blows of a hammer, the repeated word drives strong *pathos* into the minds and hearts of those who read the verse.

Verse 16 serves as the conclusion of Jude's strong, vehement words of condemnation against "certain men," that is false teachers, the apostates who infiltrated the early church. "These people are discontented grumblers, living according to their desires; their mouths utter arrogant words, flattering people for their own advantage." Jude keeps driving home the point that "these people" are unworthy of an audience. Jude's word at this climactic moment drips with satire and disdain. Consider the word he uses which is translated "grumblers." The word is Γογγυσταί. This is an example of *onomatopoeia*, a word which

---

[197] Bauckham, "Jude, 2 Peter," 88.

gives its meaning by its very sound. BDAG defines it as an "utterance made in a low tone of voice, behind-the-scenes talk."[198] Jude's use of words for emotive impact reveal rhetorical skill and divine revelation.

His statement that they use boastful words for their own selfish gain seem to have as their goal to create an "ah ha" moment for his audience and an expose of the unworthy intentions of those who have slipped into the early church.

As previously stated, the two middle paragraphs in Jude's letter are to be considered in light of the first (vv. 1-4) and the final (vv. 17-25) paragraphs. Failure to do so leads to a misinterpretation of Jude's *logos*. Placing emphasis upon the *pathos* of the middle paragraphs in isolation from that of the first and final paragraphs leads to an incorrect understanding of Jude's *ethos* and the intention of the letter as a whole.

Jude 17-25

Verse 17 begins the longest passage paragraph in Jude's letter. Some prefer to include verses 17-19 in the previous paragraph. However, the repetition of ἀγαπητοί in verses 17 and 20, plus the use of the coordinating conjunction Δέ in both verses seems to tie them together in this final paragraph.

The recurrence of the word "dear friends" (the writer prefers "beloved") encloses all Jude says in the middle sections of his letter with the warm arms of Christian compassion and concern.

Jude calls for remembrance of previous predictions of the apostles who spoke of the fact that "In the end time there will be scoffers living according to their own ungodly desires." Though in verse 18, Jude refers to the end-time scoffers, the overall emphasis shifts from "these people" to "you, dear friends." The remembering Jude has in mind does not merely address mental recollection. Rather, the meaning has to do with taking the words to heart and allowing one's self to be directed by them.

Verse 19 gives another triad exposing the negative marks of "these people." They "create divisions and are worldly, not having the Spirit." Jude clearly builds to an emotional climax relative to the apostates who slipped into the fellow-

---

198 Danker, Bauer, Arndt, and Gingrich, *Greek-English Lexicon of the New Testament*, 629.

ship of believers. Good rhetorical strategy suggests doing so. Witherington refers to Cicero's advice that "one should play the trump card last . . . (that he) should use the most outstanding and unimpeachable resource in the peroration, in this case the prophecy of Jesus and the teaching of the apostles based on it is that resource."[199]

Pathos interpretation provides assistance here. Jude appeals to the emotions of the audience by creating positive ones toward himself and apostles' prediction. He likewise creates negative ones in relation to the false teachers.

"But you, dear friends, . . ." in verse 20 turns the attention to believers and Jude's exhortations to them. Verses 20-21 contains several helpful instructions for believers living in apostate days, then and now. Grammatically, the use of the imperative "keep yourselves" (Τηρήσατε) provides the stack pole verb around which several present tense middle participles are wrapped. "As you build yourselves up (ἐποικοδομοῦντες) in your most holy faith, praying (προσευχόμενοι) in the Holy Spirit . . . waiting expectantly (προσδεχόμενοι) for the mercy of our Lord Jesus Christ for eternal life." Building toward the emotional climax there bursts forth intensity of admonition. This one imperative ("keep yourselves") and three present-tense participles ("build . . . praying . . . waiting . . .") stylistically call forth strong emotions.

Verses 22-23 turn Jude's audience to their evangelistic task. Not only do they have responsibilities relative to themselves, they also have responsibilities toward "others." (Could this "others" include even the false teachers?) Though difficult to interpret as to its *logos*, this evangelistic appeal is filled with *pathos*. The believers must recognize they are involved in a divine rescue mission.

Watson notes that in verses 22-23, "Jude uses *epanaphora* (repetition of a word or phrase at the beginning of successive clauses) in the ὅυς μέν . . . ὅυ δέ . . . ὅυς δέ structure which amplifies and emphasizes the exhortations."[200] Such repetition enhances the *pathos* of the call to evangelize.

Jude's use of emotion-laden words in verses 22-23 provides graphic pictures to persuade his audience. "Have mercy on those who waver . . ." (the use of the present tense (carries the idea of continual compassionate concern).

"Save others by snatching them from the fire" (ἁρπάζοντες). Just the use of the words fills the heart with excitement and joy. What an exhilarating

---

199 Witherington, *Letters and Homilies for Jewish Christians*, 627.
200 Watson, *Invention, Arrangement, and Style*, 75.

picture of "Rescue the perishing, care for the dying, snatch them in pity from sin and the grave" (Fanny J. Crosby, 1869).

"Have mercy on others but with fear, hating even the garment defiled by the flesh." χιτῶνα, translated "garment," was an article of clothing worn next to the body. This would be similar to today's underclothing. Now, the language becomes very loaded with *pathos*. The verb ἐσπιλωμένον translated "defiled" refers to human excrement.

Language could hardly be more *pathos* laden. The picture elicits a number of reactions from the senses: the foul odor of human excrement, the sight of a soiled garment. Schreiner says, "Such a picture shocks the readers with how polluting and corrupting sin is."[201] Then, to the point, he adds, "Furthermore, believers need to beware of getting too entangled with some who sin, lest the sinner influence them rather than vice versa."[202] To this, we add the statement of Watson: This is hyperbole . . . (which) graphically depicts the severity of even the smallest amount of exposure to sin and the foul nature of contamination by sin."[203]

Jude closes his letter with an outburst of praise. Verses 24-25 contain this final doxology. He begins by an ascription of praise to God for His mighty deeds. Jude exclaims, "Now to Him who is able . . . to keep . . . make you stand . . ." Every word in this most glorious doxology flows with grateful emotion. Jude concludes with heartfelt praise for who God is. He climbs the mountain of emotion with a series of honor words. There could hardly be a more emotional conclusion to Jude's letter. The closing flourish celebrating God's "glory, majesty, power, and authority . . ." sounds the trumpets of an emotional herald to God's great person.

There can be little doubt that Jude, under the inspiration of the Holy Spirit, consciously chooses the words of his doxology to provide for an appropriate conclusion to his discourse and lead his audience into a heartfelt worship service of "the only God and our Savior . . . Jesus Christ our Lord."

Jude puts the finishing touches on the doxology and the entire letter by thrusting the audience into the dimensions of eternity—"before all time, now and forever. Amen!"

---

201 Schreiner, "1, 2 Peter, Jude," 489.
202 Ibid.
203 Watson, *Invention, Arrangement, and Style*, 76.

Chapter Five

Using *Pathos* in Sermon Delivery of Preaching Paragraphs

The proclamation of gospel truth constitutes the ultimate goal of biblical exegesis. Paul's often-used statement, "Therefore, since we know the fear of the Lord, we try to persuade people" (2 Cor 5:11) serves as a guiding aspiration for all gospel proclamation. Those who teach and preach the Word of God must always have this as their ultimate purpose relative to those to whom we minister. As to people, the purpose is to bring the lost to faith in Jesus Christ and help believers grow in their faith. As to God, the ultimate purpose is to bring honor and praise and glory to Him.

These ultimate purposes must provide guidance so that there will be a God-intended persuasion, not an unacceptable manipulation. Speaking of this distinction Hogan and Reid warn, "Of the three means of persuasion *pathos* is the most open to blatant manipulation. Without a balanced interest in *logos* and *ethos*, *pathos* can easily slide into dangerous preoccupation of creating effect for effect's sake."[204]

Believing this to be true, the writer's purpose in this monograph intends to point all exegetes to the *pathos* of a given Scripture passage itself. A distinction between this and the *pathos* of the person seeking to persuade makes possible legitimate persuasion. Ideally, the *pathos* of one's selected passage should become the *pathos* of the speaker. This may not always be the case, but it should be the goal. Primacy should be given to the intention to incarnate Scripture *pathos* rather than allow the often opposite and contradictory emotions of the

---

[204] Hogan and Reid, *Connecting with the Congregation*, 86.

one who proclaims Scripture. P. T. Forsyth reminds us that we must always be aware that the Bible is first "the supreme preacher to the preacher."[205]

In the course of praying over and studying a Scripture pericope, the preacher will draw close to its *pathos*. Scripture must always be approached in a spirit of prayer. The same Holy Spirit who inspired humans to write Scripture will enable preachers to understand it. The necessity of approaching the exegetical assignment with a prayerful spirit must always be acknowledged. Further, the first emotional overtones of a biblical preaching paragraph should be carefully observed. Just what emotions come forth from the passage? How does the passage make one feel? Record those emotional triggers. Doing this will help in internalizing the mood of Scripture within the preacher. Such an exercise will go far in assisting one to look toward transferring them to an audience.

This writer has often said, "A message that is 'born' in the study is more likely to be 'born again' in the pulpit, regardless of our competing emotions."[206] The goal of James S. Stewart should be ours. It was said of him that he would "start expounding on a subject . . . then get so carried away . . . that it began to take control of him . . . there would be an increase in emotional intensity and a crescendo of descriptive detail and lyrical expression."[207]

Fortunately, those who exegete the *logos* and *pathos* of Scripture have a communication power upon which to draw that does not assist others in secular attempts at persuasion. The same Holy Spirit who inspired human authors to write down Scripture content wrapped in emotional texture promises to assist human communicators in their efforts. Holy Spirit illumination will not be contrary to Holy Spirit inspiration. The Spirit's inspiration gives specific, punctiliar revelation within the confines of biblical canon. The Spirit's illumination may be called upon to enable correct interpretation and communication of the *logos* and *pathos* of Scripture as revealed. Such finds expression in many New Testament passages (ex., 1 Thes 1:5; 1 Cor 2:4; Eph 1:17, etc.).

---

205 Forsyth, P. T., *Positive Preaching and the Modern Mind* (Grand Rapids: Eerdmans, 1964), 11.

206 Vines and Dooley, *Passion in the Pulpit,* 148.

207 Larsen, David L., *The Company of the Preachers: A History of Biblical Preaching from the Old Testament to the Modern Era* (Grand Rapids: Kregel, 1998), 771.

The New Testament promises that the Holy Spirit will provide aid to accurately and passionately preach the Word. David Wells says, "The preacher comes with God's own self-disclosure; the orator came simply with skills that moved on the audience."[208] This writer wrote previously, "When the Holy Spirit takes over, He will help us preach the passion of the Scripture passage and keep our competing emotions from overshadowing the divinely inspired *pathos* of the Word He inspired."[209] Thus may the preacher avoid preaching his own self-generated *pathos* and preach the tone of the Scripture passage instead.

Such careful interpretation of Scripture pericopes will have a positive effect on the intended persuasion. To correctly convey the *pathos* of Scripture itself rather than one's own *pathos* at the moment of proclamation enables one to avoid illegitimate manipulation. Scripture passages not only have a content component which must be explained. They also have a tone element that must be communicated. This suggests that the messenger of Scripture should no more fail to adequately preach its *pathos* than he would fail to give expression to its *logos*. To do so opens one up to the danger of unbiblical manipulation.

This chapter draws closer to demonstrating the importance of interpreting how a Scripture paragraph is communicated as well as the delivery of what is said. The chapter will address the subject of using the *pathos* found in the Jude preaching paragraphs in actual delivery. As will be expressed here, certain means drawn from communication theory are available in making specific efforts to reflect the *pathos* of a Scripture passage.

In his volume *Nonverbal Communication*, UCLA Professor Albert Mehrabian suggests three fundamental elements that influence the persuasive effectiveness of what one says by addressing how one says it. The interested reader will profit from further study of his work.[210] He says that verbal, vocal, and visual factors impact how a message is received. These three factors enhance the communication of Scripture *pathos* in addition to its *logos*.

---

208 Wells, David, "The Theology of Preaching: The Biblical World in the Contemporary World," *Journal of The Evangelical Homiletics Society* 9, No. 1 (March 2009), 24.

209 Vines and Dooley, *Passion in the Pulpit,* 149.

210 Mehrabian, Albert, *Nonverbal Communication* (New York: Routledge, 2017).

VERBAL COMMUNICATION

By the verbal factor, Mehrabian means that which has to do with the content of a message. To be sure, having something worth saying remains primary. Vocal factors assist or hinder the communication of a message. How does the speaker sound? Such variables as volume, pitch, rate, and pace work together toward effective communication. Perhaps surprising to some, visual factors, especially facial expression, the use of the eyes, gestures, and bodily movement, all contribute to the communication process. Consider how these three factors communicate as they relate to Scripture presentation.

Verbal communication remains the dominant consideration. The words of a passage of Scripture carry within themselves the verbal arguments the inspired text means to carry forward. The question now becomes, just what words will the preacher use to carry the words of Scripture to his audience? This divinely inspired truth wrapped in *pathos* must be delivered in such a manner that the listeners will be emotionally and intellectually engaged. Dooley says, "Though we cannot divorce the message from the messenger, we should aspire to speak in such a way that the substance of our sermon is emotionally engaging."[211]

John Owen catches the importance of speaking God's Word in our words: "The Word is like the sun in the firmament . . . But the preaching of the Word is as the motion and beams of the sun, which actually and effectually communicate that light and heat unto all creatures, which are virtually (essentially and energetically) in the sun itself."[212]

Warren Wiersbe illustrates the importance of one's verbal communication in his book *Imagination in Preaching*. He compares the counsel of Ahithophel and Hushai to Absalom who usurped the kingdom from his own father, King David. The story is found in 2 Samuel 17. Absalom had a decision to make. What should Absalom do about pursuing his father who had escaped into the wilderness? The two different approaches in communicating their counsel reveal the difference between mere content-oriented words and those

---

211 Vines and Dooley, *Passion in the Pulpit,* 154ff.

212 John Owen, *The Works of John Owen,* William H. Goold, Ed., 3rd Ed., Vol. 6 (Carlisle, PA: Banner of Truth, 1977), 245.

Using Pathos in Sermon Delivery of Preaching Paragraphs

filled with *pathos*. Ahithophel's counsel was straightforward and to the point (2 Sam 17:1-3). Just the facts. Hit him while he is weary. Absalom was inclined to follow that plain vanilla counsel.

Until he heard Husai's counsel. Husai fills his counsel with vivid word pictures. He compares David and his fighting men to a fierce wild bear robbed of her cubs, David as having the heart of a lion, Absalom's fighters like the dew settling on the ground (2 Sam 17:7-13). Husai paints pictures with his words. In his use of verbal pictures, Husai turns Absalom's ears into eyes. His counsel is followed by Absalom.[213]

To achieve this vividness of words, Dooley makes several helpful suggestions. Vivid verbal language in the delivery of Scripture follows the example of Scripture itself. As will be noted in the preaching paragraphs of Jude, Scripture itself abounds in such verbal vividness. This writer will draw from Jude's Spirit-inspired words to suggest vivid words in current language to convey vivid descriptions of the truth thus shared. Picturesque verbs, adjectives with flourishing oratory, metaphors and similes in the text itself will suggest ways to speak with effective verbal language. In *Power in the Pulpit*, Jim Shaddix and this writer say, "Vivid language is interesting language."[214] In this vein, colorful words and phrases enhance verbal communication. The formal word, *onomatopoeia*, refers to words that give their meaning by how they sound in speech. Phrases such as "the buzzing of the bee" may be spoken with effect. Hauser says, "When we use language in unusual ways, we attract attention to our thoughts."[215]

Further, the writer often speaks of painting pictures with words. Sermons conveying the grandeur and glory of Scripture may legitimately be transmitted in beautiful language that captures and overwhelms the heart of listeners. At other times, the writer finds that imaginary dialogue heightens the emotional impact of a biblical passage.

---

[213] Wiersbe, Warren, *Preaching and Teaching with Imagination* (Wheaton: Victor Books/SP Publications, 1994), 15-20.

[214] Vines and Shaddix, *Power in the Pulpit*, 272.

[215] Hauser, Gerard A., *Introduction to Rhetorical Theory*, 2nd Ed. (Long Grove, IL: Waveland, 2002), 233.

Dooley also includes pithy statements as helpful in giving verbal expression to biblical *pathos*. The writer will use examples from paragraph sermons in the book of Jude. Though Dooley correctly cautions that this may be overdone, he indicates that careful use of pithy statements may enhance good emotive content. In a similar manner, well-known quotes from familiar literature or current highly visible quotes may profitably communicate the emotion of a biblical text. Dooley cites Charles Dickens' "It was the best of times; it was the worst of times" as an example. He indicates that using such quotes triggers emotional responses in the listeners.[216]

Though Dooley makes other suggestions, we will turn our attention to the Jude paragraphs. He says that provoking comparisons enhances verbal communication. He further suggests that sermon illustrations may be used to make these kinds of comparisons.[217]

Dooley pulls from the rhetorical box yet another tool in effective verbal communication. Repetition may be effective. Repetition enables the preacher to move along the *pathos* of a passage by using a rising sense of emotion as a means to hold attention.[218]

Other means to share the truths of Scripture passages are carefully placed stories and humor. This writer has the experience of many others who preach the Word. Often listeners share their recall of stories the writer told in a message rather than other parts of the message. Care must be taken that the stories communicate the same *pathos* of the passage the story intends to convey.[219]

Another helpful tool in text-driven preaching of its *pathos* is the use of humor. While caution must be taken that humor be appropriately used, there are times when humor provides a welcome relief when dealing with such emotion-laden passages as those found in the book of Jude. Audiences should not be gripped in highly dramatic emotional modes throughout a message without some relief. Humor along the way provides that relief.

---

216   Vines and Dooley, *Passion in the Pulpit*, 155-156.
217   Ibid., 159.
218   Ibid., 160.
219   Ibid., 161.

Using Pathos in Sermon Delivery of Preaching Paragraphs

VOCAL COMMUNICATION

Preachers of the Word of God have their own, distinct vocal equipment. Some have rich, resonant voices. Others have tinny, high octave ones. These vocal characteristics may be used with telling effect. This does not mean vocal qualities are beyond improvement. Nor does it mean that vocal variety cannot be improved. To this end, care should be taken that tonal quality does not contradict the emotive thrust of biblical content. This writer believes every communicator of divine truth will be benefited by vocal training.

This writer previously noted, "The vocal sounds that reach our listeners' ears are crucial to their understanding the *pathos* of our preaching passage."[220] Thomas Watson said, "It was by the ear, by our first parents listening to the serpent, that we lost paradise; and it is by the ear, by hearing of the Word preached, that we get to heaven."[221]

The importance of discerning the emotive meaning of a biblical passage becomes very practical at this point. This becomes the key ingredient in adequate communication of biblical *pathos*. Kuhn says Bible interpreters must "explore what sorts of dispositions the biblical author is seeking to cultivate in his readers throughout an entire book . . ."[222] Once the preacher deciphers that *pathos*, the further step of determining how best to deliver the *pathos* as well as *logos* of said passage becomes paramount. The question should be addressed: "How best can I move the hearts of my audience as well as inform their minds?"

This writer encountered the importance of vocal communication in 2 Chronicles 18. The prophet Micaiah was speaking before Kings Jehoshaphat and Ahab. When asked if they should go to war, Micaiah says (paraphrased), "Sure thing. Go up and the enemies will fall before you." Sounds pretty good, doesn't it? But, Ahab detects a sarcasm in the prophet's voice. He responds, "How many times do I have to tell you to speak the Lord's truth?" Then, Mic-

---

220 Vines and Dooley, *Passion in the Pulpit*, 177.
221 Bickel, *Light and Heat*, 12.
222 Karl Kuhn, *The Heart of Biblical Narrative: Rediscovering Biblical Appeal to the Emotions* (Minneapolis: Fortress Press, 2009), 143.

aiah shoots straight with him, "I see Israel scattered like sheep without a shepherd . . ." There is something vocally in the way he says it.

As shall be demonstrated in the next section, the importance of visual communication carries great weight. But, the tone of our voices as we articulate biblical truth sets the stage for the audience to sense that one's visual presentation matches the words. Dooley succinctly puts it: "Content instructs the vocal packaging and the vocal advises the visual countenance."[223]

Care in preparing how to deliver the *logos* and *pathos* of a biblical passage reaps great dividends in the effective communication of the same. Such care enables the communicator to avoid several pitfalls in delivery. The death knell of effective delivery, a monotone vocal delivery, will be avoided when the preacher takes time to match the vocal expressions with the content and emotion found in a textual package. Too much polish in delivery may be avoided when the vocal delivery parallels the passage itself. Such avoids calling attention to the beauty of the vocal presentation rather than the substance of the passage.

Four vocal couplets properly integrated go far to enable the speaker to effectively transfer biblical content and emotion through the speaker to the audience.[224]

Rate and pace. Rate indicates the speed with which we speak, that is, the number of words spoken divided by the time elapsed. Pace has to do with the flow of our speaking. It gives the sense of movement in the delivery. Pace lets the listeners know we are going somewhere. An understanding of the *pathos* of a passage serves to give helpful guidance as to rate and pace.

Volume and stress. Volume has to do with how loud or soft our speech may be. Loud and soft may be effective in delivering the *pathos* of a Scripture passage. Stress speaks of the intensity or force used to emphasize certain words. Word emphasis is the purpose of stress.

Pitch and inflection. Pitch involves the movement of the voice up and down one's vocal scale. The melody of one's voice finds expression in pitch. Inflection goes more to the change of pace within a syllable or word. Good

---

[223] Vines and Dooley, *Passion in the Pulpit,* 169.

[224] Vines and Shaddix, *Progress in the Pulpit,* 283-311. Jim Shaddix and this writer have a chapter that gives guidance in understanding how to apply good vocal strategy to these couplets. See chapter 8, "Playing the Voice," pp. 283-311.

inflection suggests asking a question, spewing sarcasm, declaring conviction, indicating doubt, etc.

Phrases and pauses. Grouping words into units of thought constitutes phrasing. A phrase might well be described as units of thought bound by pauses. Pauses serve as the periods, commas, and exclamation points of speech. Pauses serve as friends of those who desire to communicate scriptural meaning. A pause may indicate shock, emphasis, thoughtfulness, etc.

All of these vocal variables, properly used, assist one in communicating the *pathos* of a biblical passage. For just one example, consider variety in volume. If the passage carries tenderness, soft volume does the job. If the passage suggests excitement or agony or pain, loud volume should be the tone. Spurgeon colorfully states the case: "A preacher can commit ministerial suicide by harping on one string, when the Lord has given him an instrument of many strings to play upon."[225]

The writer notes the tendency of some, especially younger preachers, to consciously or unconsciously imitate the vocal delivery of favorite preachers. This common affliction was not avoided by this writer. Perhaps natural tendencies in this direction afflict most when they begin the ministry of preaching the Word. However, these tendencies should be noted and assiduously avoided.

One of the most effective in the use of vocal delivery in our times was Martin Luther King, Jr. Jeffrey Edwards says of King: "The gradual ascendancy of his pitch from a low growl at the beginning of the sermon to a piercing shout at the upper range of his high baritone, the predictable rhythm of the rise and fall of his voice, and the relentless increase in the rate of his speech—all contribute to the melodiousness, the songlike quality of his voice."[226]

These suggestions for vocal variety have application for every aspect of the communicative process. The thrust at this point, however, relates more to the effective delivery of Scriptural *pathos*. Vocal communication helps or hinders in the transmission of biblical *pathos*. Dooley says, "Mastering these vocal guidelines will help us to fade into the background as much as possible as we embody the spirit of our text . . . Keeping the text central means that we

---

[225] Spurgeon, Charles, *Lectures to My Students* (London: Marshal, Morgan, & Scott, 1954), 170.

[226] Edwards, "The Literary Structure of Jude," 133.

hide behind our Scripture rather than vice versa. Doing so will evoke the same tone in our listeners that they hear reverberating in us."[227] Keeping these vocal variables in mind and using them appropriately will enable one to move his audience with the Spirit-intended passion.

VISUAL COMMUNICATION

Albert Mehrabian's classic study analyzed the effectiveness of the three communication factors as to the believability they generate in an audience. Verbal communication constitutes 7% effectiveness, 38% of vocal communication, and 55% of visual communication is tied to audience effectiveness.[228] Clearly, the visual component carries the most weight as to the believability and persuasiveness of a speaker, which leads one to the inevitable conclusion: When a speaker's visual communication contradicts his verbal and vocal factors, the visual tends to prevail.

This does not overshadow the importance of the content of a selected biblical passage nor its inherent *pathos*. Rather, the need is to be sure visual communication neither contradicts nor overshadows the *logos* and *pathos* therein. Having recognized this, the importance of visual communication should be noted. An example of this becomes apparent in the passage where the words say Jesus looked upon Peter who had just denied Him. What kind of look was it? Was it one of anger? No! Rather, this writer takes the view that it was a look of wounded love and appeal. In communication of this, the preacher can use his eyes, his facial expression, and even his gestures and movement of his body.

A wide variety of visual communication aspects should be considered. The messages of the eyes, the expressions on the face, the gestures of the hands, and the movements of the body all play a part in effective visual communication. None of these should contract the content and emotive mode of the biblical passage. Rather, they should all be factors in transmitting biblical *pathos* to the audience. One should not glare with the eyes while communicating tenderness and love. Expressions of joy on the face should not be seen when talking about the

---

227 Vines and Dooley, *Passion in the Pulpit*, 176.
228 Ibid., 152. See *Passion in the Pulpit*, p. 152 for a chart depicting this study.

horrors of hell. The hands should not be extended in invitation when communicating about rejection. The body should not be running across the platform when talking about the importance of being alone with God in morning devotions.

Many who proclaim Scripture seem to have a natural inclination to use visual communication correctly. But careful study of the *pathos* of a biblical passage will suggest ways that such visual signaling will be greatly enhanced. Dooley suggests that planning visual *pathos* has legitimacy and gives helpful guidelines. He says, "Following the inspired *pathos* throughout the passage and demonstrating it for your people will unveil the heart of the pericope, along with its truth."[229]

The eyes may be used to communicate *pathos*. The often-used statement, eyes are the window to the soul, indicates this. One's eyes are the most expressive members of our body. Eye contact enables the speaker to sense the understanding and mood of the audience; it also enables the audience to grasp the spirit of what is being said. The preacher should ask of his text just what kind of eye contact will be the most helpful to good communication.

Facial expression helps drive home the content and emotion of Scripture. An infinite variety of emotion finds rich expression on the face. The scowl of displeasure, the uplifted face of ecstasy, the dark brooding of unhappiness, and the upward and backward nods of anticipation all serve as messengers of *pathos*. The preacher should seek from the Scripture passage the appropriate facial expressions to helpfully convey its message. Just what message does the preacher intend? Does the passage communicate joy? Then let the face communicate that. Does the passage communicate anger? Then let the face communicate that.

Gesture and body movement probably are the easiest to abuse. This writer often discourages the planning of either. Further, the writer discourages imitating one's preaching heroes in gesture and movement. Dooley suggests there is value in planning some gestures and body movements. A rather large speaking room often calls for more pronounced gestures and an increase in body movement.

Similar to what has been noted above, the use of gesture and body movement may consciously or unconsciously imitate popular speakers. Again, the appeal—note these imitations and take care to eliminate them. Gesture and

---

[229] Vines and Dooley, *Passion in the Pulpit*, 183ff.

body movement should reflect one's own personality and style of presentation, not that of an admired preacher.

Moving forward, the focus of the chapter will be upon using Mehrabian's three fundamental elements that increase the effectiveness of what one says by how one says it. They function as components of a helpful algorithm to assist the expositor of Scripture in delivering Scripture *pathos* to an audience. These will be applied to the primary preaching paragraphs the writer has enumerated in the book of Jude. These comments will not be exhaustive, but rather will be suggestive. To seek to examine every verse, phrase, word, etc. of the entire book would be beyond the limits of this monograph. The result would be a commentary. In the conclusion, the writer will present the case for the need to provide commentaries that will include such insights from the *pathos* of Bible books.

The writer also recognizes that the suggestions of *pathos* interpretation as related to delivery in Jude's preaching paragraphs come from this writer's own particular personality, selection inclinations, and delivery style. Others may see the *pathos* of these preaching paragraphs with their own interpretive eyes. Matters of differences of interpretation as to the *pathos* that needs to be conveyed in the delivery of Jude's pericopes do not inhibit such attempts, but rather encourages the widest possible opinions and suggestions. Such variety enriches biblical interpretation. It opens up the possibility of new and exciting exegetical endeavor which should lead to better communication of biblical truth.

JUDE 1-4

Verbal Communication

As one approaches delivery of a series of sermons from Jude, there is the immediate awareness that Jude himself uses a great deal of vivid verbal language. Gilmore quotes Origen: "Origin . . . rightly spoke of Jude: it is 'full of strong words of heavenly grace though it be a few lines in length.'"[230] Gilmore adds: "When you read Jude expect to be jolted, expect to be revived, expect to have

---

230 Gilmore, *Sick Crack or Sound Crick?*, 20.

your heart beat of what a Christian should be and believe restored."[231] Watson says, "The emotional response or *pathos* that Jude desires to elicit from his audience in the peroration (is) extreme urgency and dust. He elicits *pathos*, not by the use of explicit emotional appeal . . . but by vivid emotive words, such as 'pervert,' 'licentiousness' . . ."[232]

This becomes obvious in the opening verses. Because of this, the expositor has little need to go beyond Jude's word selection. These divinely inspired words may be made more vivid with brief explanation and illustration. For instance, the word "called" reminds of the parable of Jesus to which people were "called." (The CSB translates, "invited," Luke 14:16.) The quote from Spurgeon provides color—"It is a good thing God chose me before I was born because He surely would not have afterwards."

The language of the introductory verses after the brief introduction in verses 1-2 invites more verbal vividness. A key term "Dear friends" (the writer prefers "Beloved") suggests warm *pathos*. A familiar couplet may be used: "How Thou couldst love a wretch like me and be the God thou art, is darkness to my intellect but gladness to my heart" (source unknown). The phrase "contend for the faith" (v.3) calls up pictures of warfare. This phrase might vividly communicate meaning: Jude puts down the harp, and picks up the trumpet. Or, this one: Jude suddenly hurls a thunderbolt!

Jude's word selection relative to the inroads "some people" (the apostates) have made among God's people conveys a vivid picture. Jude says they "have come in by stealth" (v. 4). Background pictures of the word provide comparison and illustration. The word could refer to an alligator, subtly, secretly, sliding into water to head toward its victim. Comparisons make the word come alive. To communicate to modern audiences the simile of islamic terrorists may convey the emotive mood.

The concluding part of verse 4 has reference to these ungodly people who pervert God's grace as an excuse for vileness—"turning the grace of our God into sensuality." Use of alliterative phrases assist in communicating the emotional mode of the phrase: They turn liberty into license, grace into disgrace. A timely quote from John Calvin may be used: "It is bad to live under

---

231 Gilmore, *Sick Crack or Sound Crick?*, 20.
232 Watson, *Invention, Arrangement, and Style*, 39.

a prince who permits nothing, but much worse to live under one who permits everything."[233] Further, any number of illustrations from modern culture are available and may serve to present the truth of Jude's language with effective verbal communication.

The writer reminds again that such matters become highly selective based on the particular personality and means of verbal expression of the individual expositor. The opening paragraph lends itself to a wide variety of verbal communicative strategies.

Vocal Communication

The use of several vocal variables in delivery provide the preacher with opportunities to deliver the opening paragraph of Jude with effectiveness. Rate and pace are fairly easy going in one's opening remarks. Just a moderate speed and a sense that the message is going somewhere should be established in the opening remarks. When Jude indicates serious business must be handled that causes him to move from calmer, more pleasing subjects like "the salvation we all share," the rate should be quickened.

At this point, also, the volume might be elevated and "contend for the faith . . ." could be given special stress. The same variation might be applied when speaking of those who "come in by stealth." Rather then increased volume, the phrase might be used with lower volume. Then, the volume might be lifted again when communicating about the "ungodly" who are "turning the grace of our God into sensuality." Applying stronger stress to "ungodly" and "sensuality" has communicative value.

Grouping certain words together into phrases enhances the communicative endeavor. Well-placed pauses also serve one well. Consider just the opening statement about believers as "the called." A brief pause after this word serves to point forward to several key phrases. "Loved by God the Father" and "kept for Jesus Christ" are phrases that communicate effectively. A pause between them also enhances effective emotional content.

---

233 Charles W. Colson, *Kingdom in Conflict* (Grand Rapids: Zondervan Publishing Company, 1987), 205.

Another place where use of pause can grip the audience is in verse 3. Talking about the salvation believers share Jude suddenly turns to a pressing problem that calls for immediate attention. The faith must be contended for! Ungodly people have stealthily creeped into the fellowship, bringing disturbing doctrinal and moral deviation! Watson says that "Quintilian advises that it is sometimes necessary to frighten the audience in the exordium in order to gain desired objectives . . . (to create) anxiety to stir up hope and fear . . . (to bring about) a sense of urgency."[234]

Visual Communication

Visual presentation of this opening paragraph will greatly benefit the preacher as he seeks to transfer the emotive mood of the Scripture passage from his heart to that of his audience. In the opening verses the eyes can create unity between preacher and people as he quickly moves through familiar terminology to the average audience of believers. Looking at various parts of the room assist to this end. Moving into the issue at hand the eyes may communicate concern, alarm and distress. Even touches of anger may flash from the eyes as the expositor recounts the intrusion of those who stealthily bring in immoral teachings to the fellowship of believers.

Facial expression will reflect the varying emotional messages Jude's letter delivers. Joy and appreciation should be indicated with appropriate facial expression. Then, the face becomes reflective of the seriousness of the alarming development Jude discusses. Care should be taken that the facial expressions should be appropriate to the subject at hand. Perhaps the preacher will be helped by imagining how Jude's facial expressions changed as he delivered the opening paragraph to a live audience. Further, some help concerning the expressions of surprise and shock that may have been manifested on the faces of his listeners.

The writer has some hesitancy to suggest any particular gestures in the presentation of this opening preaching paragraph. Gestures are very personal and expressive of the unique style of each expositor of Bible truth. The counsel to be natural in one's use of gesture, rather than rehearsed has merit. Perhaps in the course of the opening verses few gestures should be the approach. As the

---

234 Watson, *Invention, Arrangement, and Style*, 39.

subject becomes more serious the hands might seek to picture the silent, secretive invasion of apostate teachers.

Body movement probably should follow the approach recommended as to gesture on the part of each person who seeks to communicate the truths found here. There doesn't seem to be the need for excessive movement in the opening verses. As the serious problem comes forth there might be some movement toward the audience to draw them in to the matter at hand. There could even be some moving to the side then moving forward to illustrate the transporting of error into the church.

JUDE 5-10

Verbal Communication

This section begins Jude's main body of discussion. Jude's concern comes to the forefront. His words are precise, picturesque, and telling. The skill Jude demonstrates indicates his knowledge of methods of rhetorical persuasion. The words brim with color. The expositor may confine himself to the words of the text and communicate verbally the *pathos* of Jude's paragraph. Consider a few of these words and their emotive content.

The contrast between the words "saved" and "destroyed" in verse 5 gives rich pictures of the joy of salvation and the grief of divine judgment. "Eternal chains in deep darkness" are filled with *enargia* that create pictures in the minds of those who hear or read them.

As an example, consider Jude's inclusion of the dispute between Michael the archangel and the devil (vv. 9-10). The words Jude uses conveys what Watson calls the "*pathos* of startled disbelief by observing that even the archangel Michael acted only in accord with a higher moral authority."[235]

The observant reader will immediately sense a heightened level of seriousness in this paragraph. Though verse 4 indicates a real danger facing believers, this should not cause one to forget the expressions of warmth, fellowship, and concern for truth found in the opening paragraph. However, this preaching

---

235 Watson, *Invention, Arrangement, and Style*, 55-56.

paragraph begins a rather intense discussion of false teachers who are infusing the body of Christ with dangerous spiritual disease. So the question—just what words should be used to communicate this danger?

Introductory words to this section perhaps will be aided by vivid illustrations demonstrating the reality of the danger. This writer used the illustration of Jim Jones, who led the People's Temple cult in a massive suicide at Guyana in 1978. From this, an easy transition is made to the three historical events Jude uses to illustrate the damning effects of apostasy. Color words in recounting and applying them provide help in drawing the emotional mode here.

As the writer has indicated, Jude's words themselves paint pictures that convey *pathos*. Other color words selected by the exegete may be added to enhance *pathos* communication. In discussing Jude's statement about God's judgment upon these historical examples of apostasy, the use of alliteration can be helpful. Consider its use in summary: "When society passes laws to condone unnatural acts, it is ripe for judgment. When such is permitted, protected and promoted, judgment is on the way."

Vocal Communication

Vocally, the paragraph may be communicated by use of several of the vocal variables. Perhaps the paragraph calls for a slow, deliberate rate and pace. Though the desire is to indicate the passage is going somewhere, there should be a conscious effort to spend a proper amount of time on its various elements, thus an appropriate rate is desirable.

A rising and then declining volume at appropriate places in the exposition communicates meaning. For instance, the sexual immorality and perversions of the passage call for a degree of increased volume. Then the judgment that was theirs is communicated by a softer, more somber sound.

Good pitch and inflection in the delivery of various parts of the paragraph enable the preacher to transfer the *pathos* of the passage to the audience. Rising pitch as each historical illustration receives attention gives the sense of the emotional mood of deep sinfulness and severe judgment. Inflection of words communicates *pathos*. Apply inflection to words such as "abandoned" in verse 6 or "rebuke" in verse 9.

THE VITAL ROLE OF *PATHOS*
IN A COMPLETE TEXT-DRIVEN INTERPRETATION OF THE BOOK OF JUDE

Good phrasing and pause serve well to enhance vocal presentation. The punctuation of verse 10 in the Christian Standard Bible actually does it for the expositor. The use of pause at this point followed by a vocal expression of disgust and condemnation can create the negative response of fear and shame the Holy Spirit intends by the words given to Jude.

The phrase, "And what they do understand by instinct" is one unit of thought. "By these things they are destroyed" is another. The first ends with a helpful pause. Preparation for the final phrase receives assistance by means of the pause before it. And the pauses serve to highlight the middle phrase, "like irrational animals."

Visual Communication

The eyes may effectively communicate the *pathos* of this somber portion of Jude. The eyes will not twinkle; they will rather communicate concern, severity, and awe. The face should not have a silly grin but, rather, a picture of seriousness.

Gestures should not be unconstrained and out of control. Each gesture should communicate the methodical presentation of deep sin and certain judgment Jude intends to highlight. Body movement that is slow and deliberate might signal the somber message of this paragraph.

JUDE 11-16

The intensity of *pathos* in this third passage paragraph builds like the cascading of mighty waters rushing down a mountainside. *Pathos* overflows as Jude's letter reaches a strong climax of meaning and intensity.

Verbal Communication

Though some affix verse 11 to the previous paragraph, this writer has chosen to have it preface Jude's avalanche of verbal pictures in verses 12-16. The "woe" seems designed to elicit *pathos* at the beginning of the paragraph. Care should be taken at this point that the exegete does not view the use of the word as to-

Using Pathos in Sermon Delivery of Preaching Paragraphs

tally negative. Reference should be made to the familiar uses of the word by the Lord Jesus Christ. Surely, He uses the word, not in an outburst of anger, but with emotions of wounded love and sorrow at the judgment indicated by the word. The expositor may use other words such as saying that the "woe" manifests not so much a wail of denunciation as it is a cry of great sorrow.

There is a vividness of the words not apparent to the English reader. The "woe" points one toward what is ahead. Watson says, "The traditional woe formula and the three aorist verbs representing the semitic use of a prophetic perfect indicate verse 11 is a prophecy."[236]

The preacher may refer to the three Old Testament examples of apostates as three brief snapshots. The picture created by using that metaphor assists in communicating the *pathos* of the paragraph. Perhaps such a metaphor will prepare the listeners to see with great vividness the metaphors found within the text itself.

There is a rising *pathos* in the increasingly strong words used to describe the particular sins of Cain, Balaam, and Korah. "Gone . . . plunged . . . perished" are vivid and chilling. They build in intensity creating the emotion of greater concern. The preacher may use illustration to contrast the way of Cain by means of his offering to God and that of his brother, Abel. Creating illustrative content with contrast helps convey the emotion of the passage to the audience. Cain's "way" was that of the works of his hands, offering to God flowers, fruits, vegetables, spices, and grains. Abel offered an animal sacrifice. There was the stench of animal blood and the black smoke of smoldering ashes. Such language might be helpful.

The "plunging" of Balaam's error provides opportunity for vivid verbal language by its definitions. Pictures of pouring out or rushing toward suggest pictures of the swift movements toward greed that typified Balaam and many would-be prophets of the current scene. Korah's "perishing" provides a suggestive picture of the utter ruin that awaits those who rebel against the authority of God.

The expositor may enhance emotional understanding by a pithy statement comparing the sin of the three Old Testament apostates to the statement made by Jesus, "I am the way, the truth, and the life . . ." (John 14:6). Here is

---

236 Watson, *Invention, Arrangement, and Style*, 57.

the statement: "If you follow Cain, you miss the way; if you follow Balaam, you miss the truth; if you follow Korah, you miss the life."

The next word pictures in verses 12-13 vividly picture the careers of the apostates. Drawn primarily from the world of nature (the first is an exception), they arouse emotions to the point that listeners perhaps may see the scenes as happening before their very eyes. To fail to interpret the *pathos* of this stirring section robs one of effective verbal communication. Just a few of the pictures will be considered.

"They are waterless clouds carried along by winds" vividly portrays empty promises false teachers make. Let the vividness of that metaphor communicate to the audience. The illustration of the farmer, whose crops desperately need rain, sees a cloud overhead, creating anticipation. Then comes disappointment when there is no rain. This picture typifies the disappointment people experience today when they hear the claims of apostate teachers.

"They are wild waves of the sea, foaming up their shameful deeds"; graphic within itself, the picture might be communicated by using such color words as "foam and filty scum" that wash up on a seashore. Another pithy statement might be used: "The filth and shame of the inner life belches on the shores of life for all to see." "Wandering stars for whom the blackness of darkness is reserved forever." Illustrate this picture by picturing shooting stars that make a big flash, then are suddenly gone.

This series of metaphors describing the apostates broadcast their sinfulness, discredits them, and creates negative *pathos* in reference to them.

Jude's reference to Enoch in verses 14-15 conveys strong *pathos*. An interesting word usage provides vividness. The word "ungodly" is used as a noun, a verb, then an adverb. This may be communicated by saying, "Like blows of a hammer, such variety in word usage produces strong emotions."

The words of application in the paragraph (v. 16) are very vivid. The word for "grumblers" actually explains itself by the way it is pronounced. An example of *onomatopoetic* (the sound of a word that pictures its meaning). The Greek word translated "grumblers"(Γογγυσταί) has the root meaning of the cooing of doves. Pronouncing the word conveys that picture.

Vocal Communication

Rate and pace serve as useful speaking mechanisms to convey the *pathos* of this paragraph. The references to Cain, Balaam, and Korah (v. 11) may communicate the solemnity of their examples by a slow, measured pace. As the examples from nature are given (vv. 12-13), the rate may be quickened to create greater emotion in each successive picure.

Volume and stress serve the expositor well in communicating the thrust of the passage. "Woe to them!" calls for increased volume. Stress on certain words such as "dangerous reefs . . . waterless clouds . . . fruitless, twice dead and uprooted" call attention to them.

The more dramatic sections of the paragraph may be vocally communicated more effectively by moving up and down the vocal scale by rising and lowering pitch and inflection. Consider how this manifests itself by saying, "Woe" (v. 11) with a higher pitch or "discontented grumblers" (v. 16) with a lower one.

Pausing between phrases offers great assistance in communicating the emotional content of the paragraph. Again, the Christian Standard Bible in its use of punctuation assists the preacher. The phrase "trees in late autumn" receives vocal highlighting by the pause after it, just before the final phrase of the picture, "fruitless, twice dead, and uprooted."

Visual Communication

The use of the eyes offers much promise in good delivery of this Scripture passage. The eyes can communicate sorrow in the "woe" that Jude sets forth in the three Old Testament examples (v. 11). The eyes may flash with anger and strong distaste at the "dangerous reefs" that threaten God's people and "waterless clouds" that disappoint them. But the exegete must not lose sight of the controlling emotion of love that envelopes the two middle paragraphs of condemnation. The eyes surely must indicate this compassion as well.

Facial expression enhances the *pathos* of the passage in the course of the delivery. The face should not display frivolity nor silliness in this paragraph. A serious expression probably is called for in the preaching of this text.

The illustrations from nature offer some opportunities for effective gesture. Though again this writer considers them most effective when natural, consider a few opportunities for effective gesture and body movement. "Waterless clouds carried along by winds" could call for the arms to be held upward and moved from one side to the other. "Wandering stars" could be graphically displayed by gesturing with the arms overhead and falling downward, depicting the downward course of a shooting star.

Moving from one side of the platform to the other as each picture presents itself helps to bracket off each individually. The movements should probably not be hectic, but rather deliberate.

This writer again emphasizes that some of various elements involved in verbal, vocal, and visual communication often accompany those who are gifted in delivery. Those so gifted seem to naturally convey passage *pathos* indicated by these categories. However, those less-gifted may learn to use them effectively by a study of the *pathos* of a text of Scripture and a conscious effort to apply these communicative elements in the delivery of that text.

JUDE 17-25

Rhetorical terminology provides help in approaching Jude's final preaching paragraph. These final verses constitute what rhetoricians call the *peroration*, that is the concluding section of an oration. Another term, *repetitio* refers to the repetition of elements of the previous argument. Intended to recapitulate the principal points of a speech or discourse, elements of the previous parts of the speech serve as emotional impetus for the conclusion. The term *adfectus* (the arousing of emotions) provides insight as well. Jude gives evidence of understanding this aspect of the art of persuasion current in his day.

Witherington's quote from Quintilian gives direction: "In a *peroration* an orator intends to bring the discourse to a climax, summing up some of the main points (the so-called *repetitio*) and making a final emotional appeal (the *adfectus*), trying to reach the audience at the level of their deeper emotions such as love and hate, fear and trust."[237]

---

237 Witherington, *Letters and Homilies for Jewish Christians*, 627.

Edwards quotes Moo in this regard: "Vs. 17-25 restates Jude's argument using an emotional appeal . . . it may be that he naturally fell into this general style of argument as it was known to him from his surrounding culture."[238]

Verbal Communication

In his conclusion, Jude makes a smooth transition from his scathing descriptions of the apostates to positive encouragements for his "dear friends" (ἀγαπητοί). The repetition of this word from its use in verse 3 and its use again in verse 20 envelopes the entire book with positive emotions of love, compassion, and concern. The preacher will be hard pressed to verbalize in a better way than the words Jude uses. To use them clearly communicates to an audience. The overall thrust of the words used are positive and communicate effectively.

Though Jude makes reference to previous predictions and some additional statements about the characteristics of the apostates (vv. 17-19), there doesn't seem to be need for further verbal expression on the part of the preacher.

Instead, attention may be given to ways to verbalize the positive imperative "keep yourselves" (Τηρήσατε). Then, the preacher should give attention to the present participles wrapped around the imperative: "build yourselves up" (ἐποικοδομοῦντες), "praying" (Προσευχόμενοι), "waiting" (Προσδεχόμενοι). This section abounds in opportunities for effective verbal communication. Pithy statements may be used, such as: "No Bible, no breakfast," "Bible without prayer= no dynamic; prayer without Bible= no passion."

The verses speaking of seeking to win the lost (vv. 22-23) suggest many illustrations that may prove helpful in communicating Jude's evangelistic admonitions. The familiar illustration about William Booth's wire to a Salvation Army gathering should communicate: "Try tears."

The vivid picture of "snatching them from the fire" (CSB) may be enhanced by the familiar couplet of C.T. Studd: "Some want to live within the sound of church or chapel bell; I want to run a rescue shop within a yard of hell."

The danger of the one who would witness to those whose garments are stained by the filth and uncleanness of sin cries out for illustration. The writer found one that helps make this verbally effective. In the Ebola outbreak in

---

238 Edwards, "The Literary Structure of Jude," 36-37.

Sierra Leone, Dr. Sheik Umar Khan was credited with treating more than 100 victims. In the course of saving them, he contracted the virus himself and died from the disease.[239]

The concluding doxology (vv. 24-25) may be communicated with vividness by painting the picture of the different word for "keep you from stumbling" (CSB translates "protect you from stumbling") and gives an opportunity for illustration from the word being used for a surefooted horse or a good man who does not make moral lapses.

The final words of Jude really need no enhanced verbal expression. "Glory, majesty, power, and authority . . . flow with grateful, overwhelming emotion." And the concluding statement "before all time, now and forever. Amen" thrusts those who hear or read the words into a verbal symphony of praise and adoration.

Vocal Communication

These final words of Jude provide fruitful opportunities to play on the full range of vocal variables. Just a few examples should suffice. Rate and pace may come into play as there is initial reference to past predictions, repetition of some negative characteristics of the apostates. The preacher perhaps will want to move through them rather rapidly and with the sensation that one is moving to further, more meaningful matters. Then, as the admonitions are addressed, the rate may be slowed down to give time for each admonition to be considered.

Volume and stress serve well in placing emphasis on certain aspects of the final paragraph. Jude's evangelistic appeal will call for rising and falling volume. Also, stress on certain words such as "snatching . . . have mercy . . . hating . . . defiled" lends itself to effective vocal communication. The concluding doxology will create the desired emotional mood as volume and stress are used to highlight the successive statements and various words receive the necessary emphasis.

Pitch and inflection will be especially helpful in the final words of the doxology. Pronouncing each one with rising, building pitch adds to the emotional peak the Holy Spirit surely intends.

---

239   BBC News, July 30, 2014.

Phrasing and pause enhance the vocal task. For instance, the individual participial admonitions around the central admonition may be phrased together with appropriate pause between each. Likewise, the various groups who need a gospel witness may be phrased together with pauses in between them.

Visual Communication

Good eye contact becomes vital in the process of communicating the final paragraph of Jude. These verses make personal application to God's people. The preacher should look at all sections of the room, looking people in the eye. This serves to give the intended effect of drawing people personally into the encouragements given in the verses. The same effect in stating the evangelistic responsibility of God's people will be assisted with good eye contact.

Also, the flashing of the eyes as the more serious conditions of those to whom believers witness are expressed communicates effectively. And the joy and anticipation of the final glorious time when believers are in God's presence will be enhanced with eyes filled with wonder, anticipation, and joy.

The use of appropriate facial expressions provides many opportunities for good communication. In preaching the parts of the concluding paragraph that speak to doing those things necessary to stay in the atmosphere of God's love, the face should reflect determination and commitment. When speaking of those who are in need of gospel witness, let the face reflect the compassion and determination of that witness. In the concluding doxology, the face should mirror excitement and a sense of anticipation.

Though gesture and body movement in most cases during the preaching of Jude's final paragraph will come naturally, there are probably some places where thinking through how best to gesture and move will be helpful. The gesture of snatching someone from the fire might very well be planned. Moving from side to side as one discusses each kind of person who needs an evangelistic overture might be planned with positive emotional effectiveness.

In concluding this chapter, Witherington has a helpful paragraph:

> The stops must be pulled out and the emotions must be appealed to, in this case the appeal to *pathos* . . . must be more intense. The first part of

the peroration raised the level of indignation against the false teachers, whereas these verses become the *conquestio*, where the deeper positive emotions of the audience are appealed to, including the fear of losing some friends to the "fire." Thus we hear on the positive side about love, mercy, faith, hope and salvation and on the negative side about contamination, fire and judgment.[240]

---

[240] Witherington, *Letters and Homilies for Jewish Christians*, 630.

Chapter Six

Various Categories of Bible Interpretation as They Relate to *Pathos*

A part of this monograph's thesis argues that *pathos* has not received due consideration in Scripture interpretation. In that regard, this writer states in the preface: "This will be demonstrated in the widespread failure of exegetical and devotional works to give a full analysis of Scripture *pathos* in the preparation of a series of text-driven messages from the book of Jude."

In the process of research for this monograph, the writer expanded and refined the categories of biblical interpretation. This chapter will give some examination of these revised categories as they relate to Jude's letter. The chapter will be divided into (1) Linguistic and Socio-rhetorical Works, (2) Exegetical and Expository Commentaries, and (3) Devotional and Sermonic Works. Obviously, not all the research resources available for the book of Jude will receive treatment in this monograph. Such citation would be impossible to accomplish. Therefore, selected works and commentaries will serve as illustrative of the need for more attention to the emotional content of Jude and, therefore, biblical interpretation in general.

The first category is a newer understanding of the writer toward a more complete analysis of Bible study tools that assist preachers in a well-rounded interpretation. Linguistic analysis of Scripture, while a somewhat recent resource for this writer, provides excellent evaluation of the text of Jude. Further, such analysis might well serve as the fountainhead for *pathos* interpretation in the other categories of biblical interpretation. Linguists seem to recognize and anticipate this. Watson says, "Thorough rhetorical analyses of New Testament books using classical rhetoric have yet to be performed."[241]

Drawing on Watson's linguistic analysis of the book of Jude. this chapter will demonstrate that linguistic study provides a helpful spring from which other interpreters may draw refreshing waters of living biblical truth for God's people.

Socio-rhetorical study in the field of the New Testament has emerged in more recent biblical scholarship. This discipline approaches the New Testament within the context of the world in its time and the rhetorical strategies of communication at that time. Vernon K. Robbins provides a good explanation of this new approach to biblical studies. He says, "Socio-rhetorical criticism is an approach to literature that focuses on values, conviction, and beliefs both in the texts we read and in the world in which we live . . . The approach invites detailed attention to the text itself."[242] In the conclusion of his book, he says, "Socio-rhetorical criticism, then, challenges interpreters to explore a text in a systematic, broad manner that leads to a rich environment of interpretation and dialogue . . . there are all kinds of phenomena in texts that invite systematic, programmatic analysis."[243]

As to socio-rhetorical analysis, the writer will reference the groundbreaking work of Ben Witherington in providing helpful tools for exegetical/expository commentaries and devotional/sermonic works. This writer regards such works as Witherington's as a helpful step toward getting adequate *pathos* consideration in commentaries and works of Bible interpretation. The writer also applauds the current endeavors to provide commentary for various New Testament books that are now available from Witherington, *Logos*, and other sources.

The second category will involve examination of Bauckham's and Bateman's scholarly commentaries of Jude. This writer will argue that more attention to *pathos* interpretation would make their superb works even better.

---

[241] Watson, *Invention, Arrangement, and Style,* 7. Watson has an excellent discussion of the development of rhetorical criticism in biblical studies in his introduction, pp. 1ff. The writer readily acknowledges this is a new and intriguing field of study and that he has little expertise in it.

[242] Vernon K. Robbins, *Exploring the Texture of Texts: A Guide to Socio-Rhetorical Interpretation* (Valley Forge: Trinity Press International, 1996), 1.

[243] Robbins, *Exploring the Texture of Texts,* 132.

Such evaluation should not be considered as negative evaluation of their works. Rather, the writer intends that this be illustrative of the helpfulness of the study of *pathos* to a full and complete interpretation of Scripture.

The third category will be given much the same evaluation as that of the second. Devotional and sermonic works often provide the first help for preachers in text-driven preaching. Among the voluminous resources for Jude, the works of John Phillips and David Helm will be evaluated for the purposes of this monograph. The writer will argue that these excellent works could be enhanced with more attention to *pathos* interpretation.

LINGUISTIC AND SOCIO-RHETORICAL WORKS

Linguistic Works

Duane Frederick Watson's book, *Invention, Arrangement, and Style: Rhetorical Criticism of Jude and 2 Peter*, provides a resource that introduces the novice such as this writer to the linguistic analyses as they relate to complete Bible interpretation. These linguistic insights enable one to see the structure and style of the book of Jude and give indications of the same kind of helpfulness in biblical studies. Such detailed analysis, as demonstrated by Clark's in-depth analysis of the book of Jude in his *Analyzing and Translating New Testament Discourse* indicates deeper insights made possible by such a resource.

Watson defines *pathos* as applied to linguistic studies in Scripture: "*Pathos* . . . is emotion and, as a means of proof, is arousal of the emotion of the audience for or against both the matter at hand and those representing it. The rhetor seeks to elicit positive *pathos* for his own case and negative *pathos* for his opponent's case."[244] This definition and application serve well as a step toward the analysis of the emotional tone of Jude.

In the exordium (vv. 1-3) where Jude gains the attention of his audience and seeks to elicit a positive reception, Watson calls attention to Jude's use of "beloved." Not only does this provide a clear example of positive *pathos*,

---

244 Watson, *Invention, Arrangement, and Style,* 15.

but also establishes a sympathetic connection between himself and his audience.[245] For purposes of complete interpretation of Jude's main body of discourse (vv. 5-16), such positive *pathos* provides the necessary introduction to the more severe probatio. Jude seeks to persuade his audience of "the legitimacy of his case through a presentation of propositions and corresponding proofs . . ."[246] Understanding the warmth and compassion of the exordium enables the interpreter to see the severe probation through more loving eyes on Jude's part.

In the probatio (vv. 5-16), Jude "attempts to persuade the audience of the legitimacy of his case through a presentation of propositions and corresponding proofs."[247] The section abounds in numerous rhetorical devices. *Enargeia*, powerful descriptions of events and people that enable the audience to "see" what is being said, arouses *pathos* through powerful metaphors, such as dangerous reefs causing shipwreck, clouds that provide no rain and fruitless trees. *Pathos* interpretation that ties this section to the first and last ones in Jude gives the more complete picture of Jude's intention in the letter.

Moving to the peroration (vv. 17-23), Watson indicates therein the "emotional appeal of adfectus,"[248] or the exciting of the emotions. Again, Jude appeals to positive emotions for himself and negative ones for the apostate teachers. The warmth of Jude's heart finds expression in the four injunctions Jude gives his audience. Though Jude gives further negative statements toward the apostates, Watson relates that the content here contains "references to faith, prayer, God's love, Christ's mercy, eternal life, and salvation on the positive side . . ."[249]

The closing doxology (vv. 24-25) hardly suggests that Jude is bitter and angry. This closing doxology is in contrast to normal epistolary postscripts of the time. Watson wraps up his rhetorical analysis by saying, "By ending his appeal with a focus upon God, Christ, and their future hope, his audience is even more persuaded to act as Jude advises. It is an effective way to end deliberative rhetoric, and far more effective for emotional appeal than an epistolary postscript . . . (this

---

245 Watson, *Invention, Arrangement, and Style,* 38-39.
246 Ibid., 49.
247 Ibid.
248 Ibid., 67.
249 Ibid., 73.

doxology concludes) . . . exhibiting his concern that his audience not fail to see the consummation of their hopes."[250] Thus, Jude is hardly the "sick crank."

Socio-Rhetorical Works

Ben Witherington serves as our example for the more recent work being done in this field of biblical interpretation. Others, of course, might be reviewed. This writer draws from Witherington's book *Letters and Homilies for Jewish Christians: A Socio-Rhetorical Commentary on Hebrews, James and Jude*. Witherington perhaps gives us the best example of works currently underway that serve as a step between highly skilled linguistic analysis mentioned above and the commentaries and works mentioned below.

Witherington's structure for Jude remains fairly consistent with linguists who have analyzed Jude's structure. He gives the constituent elements thusly: epistolary prescript (vv. 1-2); exordium (vv. 3-4) (he locates the narration, verse 3b here as well); probatio (vv. 5-16); peroration (vv. 17-23); doxology (vv. 24-25).

Several observations give pertinent guidance. First, he notes that the narration is brief and clear, providing "a succinct statement of the facts."[251] He references Quintilian who says the narration should be "plausible in imagination . . . vehement in censure . . . vivid in description . . ."[252]

In keeping with the rhetorical style of New Testament times, Witherington calls attention to the strong probation (vv. 5-16) of Jude's epistle. He says that "Jude throws everything at them but the kitchen sink to make the audience divest themselves of these false teachers and their teachings."[253]

Witherington mentions the climax of Jude in the peroration (vv. 17-23). Jude concludes his letter by "making a final emotional appeal (the adfectus), trying to reach the audience at the level of their deeper emotions such as love and hate, fear and trust . . . (and makes) the final emotional appeal."[254] Also, he

---

250 Watson, *Invention, Arrangement, and Style*, 76.
251 Witherington, *Letters and Homilies for Jewish Christians*, 601.
252 Ibid.
253 Ibid., 607.
254 Ibid., 625.

notes that this section "references both positive (faith, prayer, God's great love, Christ's mercy, eternal life, and salvation) and negative (contamination by sin, punishment by fire) topics."[255] Witherington comes close to making the connection between the more tender inclusio (vv. 1-4; 17-25) that provides context to the more severe main body of the letter. He goes further and says that "William Brosend rightly notes the change in tone in this section which repeats the term 'beloved' concludes the discourse with a positive exhortation. He also notes an implicit synkrisis or rhetorical contrast between the false teachers and the true Christians in the audience."[256] These statements give indication that socio-rhetorical scholarship recognizes the importance of these kinds of contrasts and connections. The context of the inclusion (vv. 1-4; 17-23) also provides important understanding.

Witherington notes the importance of the peroration to the rhetorical intention of Jude. He references Cicero to the effect that "one should play the trump card last . . . that is, one should use the most outstanding and unimpeachable resources in the peroration, in this case the prophecy of Jesus and the teaching of the apostles based on it is that resource."[257]

Witherington adds another structural category when speaking of Jude's closing exhortations. He calls verses 20-23 "the conquestio, where the deeper positive emotions of the audience are appealed to . . ."[258] Again, consideration of the inclusion (vv. 1-4; 17-23) as a contextual envelope for the letter places the more severe sections of the letter in a more compassionate, loving setting.

From a socio-rhetorical standpoint, the closing doxology (vv. 24-25) receives helpful attention from Witherington. This doxology, "one of the most beautiful in the Bible," indicates to Witherington that Jude fits the category of "a sermonizing letter . . . (thus) bringing the entire letter to an emotional climax . . . (which gives Jude a) far more effective . . . emotional appeal than an epistolary postscript . . ."[259]

---

255 Witherington, *Letters and Homilies for Jewish Christians*, 626.
256 Ibid.
257 Ibid., 627.
258 Ibid., 630.
259 Ibid., 634.

The writer thinks these socio-rhetorical offerings will provide a much needed bridge to exegetical/expository commentaries and even to devotional/sermonic works.

EXEGETICAL AND EXPOSITORY COMMENTARIES

First, the extensive and detailed commentary by Richard J. Bauckham, "Jude, 2 Peter," serves as a superb exegetical guide to the biblical interpreter. In his introduction, Bauckham organizes the material around the main themes of form and structure, language, and authorship and other introductory matters. His discussion of the words used by Jude gives good direction as to their content impact. He makes reference to the catchwords Jude uses, such as "ungodly" and "kept." He also calls attention to Jude's use of typology as found in verses 5-7, 11.[260] The emotional tone conveyed by these words receives no treatment. Actually, there cannot be total separation between the *logos* of words and their *pathos*. Word themselves and their syntactical connections carry emotional impact.

Bauckham references a number of rhetorical devices, especially chiasmus that Jude employs. He makes the observation that he as well as many other exegetes note that Jude shows a fondness for triple expressions.[261] While good to note, the pleasing *pathos* thus created could provide another guide to complete exegesis.

In his section on authorship, he correctly notes the evidence in Jude's writing of rhetorical skill. He notes: "The kinds of skills he shows are the rhetorical skills which a Jewish preacher in Greek would need. Moreover, the features of good literary Greek, both vocabulary and idiom . . ."[262] The skills could have been learned from Jude reading Greek literary sources and listening to Jewish sermons. This would have been a good opportunity to call attention also to Jude's understanding of *pathos* as demonstrated in his letter.

---

260 Bauckham, "Jude, 2 Peter," 6.
261 Ibid.
262 Ibid., 26.

THE VITAL ROLE OF *PATHOS* IN A COMPLETE TEXT-DRIVEN INTERPRETATION OF THE BOOK OF JUDE

Particularly vital in understanding the overall thrust of Jude's letter warning of apostate teachers, Jude 3-4 merit special attention. Bauckham seems to indicate the importance of making a connection to the body of the letter. He says, "It is important to notice how vs. 3-4 relate to the rest of the letter."[263] At this point, the *pathos* of the introductory section could have provided a compassionate context for Jude's more severe denunciations in the main portion of Jude.

In his exegesis of this opening section, Bauckham does get close to what this writer argues should be a part of complete Scripture exegesis. He says, "Jude's purpose in seeking to demonstrate that the false teachers and their condemnation have been prophesied is not to comfort his readers with the assurance that all is happening according to God's plan . . . Still less is he indulging in mere denunciation . . . and that therefore they constitute a severe danger which Jude's readers must resist . . ."[264] Following the logical implications of that analysis toward Jude's compassionate mood here would have provided a helpful contextual embrace of the severe condemnations that follow.

Briefly, Bauckham's exegesis of the word "woe" (v. 11) would have been even more helpful by a discussion of its emotional tone as well as its content meaning. In addition, the remarkable accumulation of metaphors Bauckham references[265] could have been even more extensive should there have been noted the heightened *pathos* by Jude's use of them.

One observation as to Jude's emotional attitude toward the apostate teachers perhaps will provide greater understanding. In his discussion of the importance of witnessing, there seems to be a somewhat oblique reference to the false teachers. As Jude discusses the various groups to whom believers should witness, he makes reference to some to whom they are to "have mercy . . . with fear, hating even the garment defiled by the flesh" (v. 23). Bauckham says, "He (Jude) does not give up hope of their salvation: his readers are to continue to exercise Christian love toward them, even if prayer is now the only practical means of doing so. In these instructions Jude combines abhorrence for the sins which the false teachers are promoting and a strong belief in God's judgment on sin with a genuinely Christian concern for the reclamation of even

---

263 Bauckham, "Jude, 2 Peter," 29.
264 Ibid., 41.
265 Ibid., 79.

the most obstinate."²⁶⁶ Exactly! To tie this to the context of Jude's compassion in verses 1-4 gives a far different understanding of Jude's emotional tone in the whole letter than is often suggested.

While interesting observations concerning the *pathos* in the main body of Jude's letter could give further instances of the need for *pathos* analysis, the writer moves to the final section to sustain the argument that Jude's emotional tone in the opening and closing sections are necessary to a complete understanding of the letter.

Bauckham references the return to the word translated "dear friends" which is used again in verses 17 and 20.²⁶⁷ Not only does this repetition denote a transition in terms of content. The repetition also suggests an emotional transition as well. A discussion of Jude's mood as he closes his letter would provide context to the severe parts of the letter.

The doxology in verses 24-25 provides an ideal opportunity to give interpretation of Jude's overall emotional tone. This magnificent doxology oozes with *pathos*. One can almost sense Jude's exultation and praise. The wording of the doxology hardly suggests Jude closes out as an angry, bitter, harsh critic. Rather, the suggestion by the wording is that Jude is joyfully calling upon his audience to join him in this emotion-filled conclusion. The writer merely desires to point out that a teasing out of the *pathos* here would enhance Bauckham's commentary.

In a more recent work, *Word Biblical Themes*, Bauckham seems to be moving in a positive direction as regards *pathos* interpretation. He says, "The strong emphasis on judgment in his letter has not hardened his heart against them. It has awakened his pastoral concern for them. It combines abhorrence for the sins they are promoting, firm belief in God's judgment on sin, with a genuinely Christian desire for the reclamation of even the most obstinate."²⁶⁸

Second, consider the excellent exegetical volume by Herbert W. Bateman IV, *Evangelical Exegetical Commentary: Jude*. Bateman's massive volume gives excellent information for those who seek to interpret the meaning

---

266   Bauckham, "Jude, 2 Peter," 118.
267   Ibid., 102-103.
268   Richard J. Bauckham, *Word Biblical Themes: Jude, II Peter* (Waco: Word Books, 1990), 26.

of Jude and proclaim it to the people. There is a very helpful pattern Bateman follows for each pericope of Jude. The pattern is as follows: introduction, textual notes, translation, commentary, biblical theology comments, application, and devotional implications.

The commentary provides superior help in discerning the *logos* (content) of Jude. However, this writer discerns very little, if any, discussion of the emotional mood of any of the paragraphs. A rather extensive, but not exhaustive, survey of exegetical works on Jude leads the writer to maintain that inadequate attention to *pathos* interpretation is typical of what is found in Bateman. A few observations will be made in this regard.

Bateman organizes his commentary into introduction and commentary. As to the structure of Jude, he organizes the letter into six paragraphs (vv. 1-2, vv. 3-4, vv. 5-7, vv. 8-16, vv. 17-23, and vv. 24-25). He shows familiarity with a number of rhetorical matters. He gives a very helpful definition of inclusio: "(inclusio) is a literary framing device by which the same word or phrase occurs at both the beginning and the end of a linguistic unit."[269] Such a statement would suggest that Bateman might give some consideration of Jude's *inclusio* as to the emotional tone the *inclusio* provides. Such reference does not receive treatment.

In every paragraph Bateman discusses, he provides strong *logos* commentary. He deals not only with the *logos* content of the words Jude employs, but also the meaning conveyed by the way the letter is structured. He properly ties "beloved" in verse 3 to its reoccurrences in verses 17 and 20. Bateman approaches some *pathos* analysis when he writes "Jude's admonishing force is directed to those for whom he cares . . ."[270] Bateman indicates no effort to place the main body of Jude within the emotional tone set by verses 1-4 and verses 17-25.

He also approaches *pathos* interpretation in his comments on "woe" in verse 11 of the letter. He does tie the word used here with its use by Old Testament prophets and by our Lord. He calls the word "a rather mild reproach or perhaps even a lament in today's culture."[271] He continues by say-

---

269 Bateman, "Jude," 444.
270 Ibid., 120.
271 Ibid., 240-241.

ing, "Jude's indignation is at a peak here."[272] Bateman probably gives some indication of his own interpretation by referring to a contemporary translation of Matthew 11:21, "Damn you, Chorazin . . . and Jesus even tells Capernaum 'you'll go to hell.'"[273] This writer takes the view that Jesus did not speak those words in anger, nor did Jude, but rather, with deep compassion. The writer believes that a complete interpretation of the inclusio verses suggests a different conclusion than that of Bateman. It should be noted that Bateman rejects the use of an inclusio in Jude. He says, "Yet the simple recalling of a single word like "remember" does not an inclusio make."[274] The writer would wholeheartedly agree. But, more than a single word comes into play. The repetition of the word "beloved" also must be considered.

The compassionate references to witnessing to people in verse 23 receive no indication on Bateman's part of compassion for the apostates. The writer grants that an argument from silence should not be the major one. But the view that a more complete interpretation of verses 1-4 could serve as a setting of the emotional tone of the book, including the matter of witnessing even to those who are apostates does seem worthy of consideration.

In his commentary on the doxology, Bateman indirectly calls attention to its *pathos*. His comments cannot be read without a sense of emotional exuberance: "Doxologies are powerful statements of affirmation that are frequently used to close a worship service."[275] He closes his commentary on the whole book and primarily the doxology by quoting Pastor Tim Sprankle: "The doxology always drew a sigh of relief . . . the closing words of Jude . . . (end) with a holy exclamation point."[276]

As in previous analyses, this should in no way be viewed as a negative assessment of Bateman's superior commentary. Rather this evaluation should be considered as a suggestion that exegetical and expository commentaries would be even more helpful with commentary relative to the *pathos* of Scripture passages as well as their *logos*.

---

272 Bateman, "Jude," 241.
273 Ibid.
274 Ibid., 340.
275 Ibid., 439.
276 Ibid.

Devotional and Sermonic Works

First, John Phillips' *Exploring the Epistle of Jude* provides an example of the need for a discussion on Scripture *pathos* as well as *logos*. This is the first of the category of devotional and sermonic works that likely constitute the first sources which preachers and teachers of Scripture consult. As one would expect, Phillips gives no detailed introduction. He gives some discussion of his view as to the identity of the apostate teachers Jude exposes. Phillips takes the position that they are gnostic teachers, a view not widely held by exegetical scholars. One statement Phillips makes relative to them impacts what this writer considers to be important relative to Jude's overall atmosphere of compassion set forth in the inclusion (vv. 1-4; 17-25). He says, "But once a person embraces Gnosticism, in one or all of its manifold forms, he becomes an apostate. For such a person—as Esau discovered, as Judas learned, and as many ohers have found—there is no place for repentance."[277]

Phillips' introduction has no mention of the emotional tone Jude demonstrates in his letter. The introduction is then followed by a rather detailed, alliterative outline, which will please some and displease others. In personal discussion with Phillips, this author came to understand that his purpose in such detailed alliteration was the desire to assist the preacher at whatever text he desires to preach.

The introductory verses (1-4) talks about the word "beloved" but gives no treatment of the emotional tone the word sets for the letter, nor context it provides for the entire book. He does give further detail relative to "beloved" in its recurrence in verses 17 and 20. He properly says, "That term of endearment is for the believer, not for the apostate. It is one of the names that God gives His own."[278] Phillips had no training in linguistic analysis but does seem to instinctively communicate the *pathos* of the word. He does not, however, wrap the *pathos* of this closing section around the main body of the letter.

---

[277] John Phillips, *Exploring the Epistle of Jude* (Grand Rapids: Kregel, 2001), 10.

[278] Ibid., 7.

As to Jude's use of "woe" in verse 11, Phillips provides no indication of Jude's emotional mood. He does reference the use of the word in the Revelation but notes no tie to Jesus' use of the word. Such a reference to Jesus' use of "woe" would have provided an opportunity to consider the Lord's emotional tone by the use of the word and suggest a similar compassion on the part of Jude.

Moving to Jude's appeal to the witnessing endeavors of God's people, his words in verse 23 suggest opportunity for *pathos* analysis. Jude says, "save others by snatching them from the fire; have mercy on others but with fear . . ." Phillips' comment here is very suggestive: "Arguing is not likely to win such people. Remember that God goes after the heart. The word compassion reminds us of that fact. Often, love will find a way where logic fails. Someone has well said that we go into the kingdom of God heart first, not headfirst."[279] Such a comment brims with *pathos*. As mentioned above, though perhaps not schooled in the intricacies of *pathos* analysis, Phillips seems to grasp the *pathos* of Scripture passages.

As earlier stated, Phillips takes the view there is no hope for the apostates. Could verse 23 indicate just the opposite? The writer tends to take that view. Such statements as "have mercy" are filled with compassion and might well indicate that Jude holds out hope for the salvation of even apostates.

In the closing doxology (vv. 24-25), Phillips gets close to some *pathos* analysis. He peppers his comments concerning the same with exclamation marks.[280] He uses the exclamation point to set forth the tone of exultation and praise. Though such repetition might be considered excessive from a writing standpoint, Phillips communicates exuberant joy by this repetition. Again, perhaps Phillips gives evidence of instinctive (should we say, Holy Spirit led?) *pathos* in his comments on the doxology.

This writer has benefited greatly through the years in reading Phillips' sermonic works. The writer has no intention to minimize those benefits. Rather, in keeping with the thesis of this monograph, Phillips' works through all of the New Testament and a large portion of the Old Testament could be enhanced and provide preachers additional opportunities for complete interpretation of Scripture.

Second, David Helm's *1 and 2 Peter and Jude: Sharing Christ's Suffering* provides helpful insight for us. Helm's sermonic treatment gives a more

---

279   Phillips, *Exploring the Epistle of Jude*, 92.
280   Ibid., 95-103.

recent work (published in 2008) and thus should be expected to give evidence of an understanding of *pathos* interpretation that might not have been obvious in earlier works.

Helm's introduction briefly deals with the structure of Jude. In the brief introduction, Helm gives summary attention to the structure of the letter. He also ties Jude's admonition to contend for the faith in verse 3 to Jude's explanation of how to do that in verses 17-23. No discussions of authorship, the intended destination of the letter, nor rhetorical devices receive consideration. Such matters receive attention in the further chapters of Helm's work. The writer does not intend this as a criticism, but merely an observation. The sermonic nature of his book reflects his presentation of normal introductory items in an opening sermon to his church congregation. He gives no discussion of Jude's *logos* nor his *pathos*. The introduction would be an excellent place to call attention to the emotional tone of the letter in terms of its content and also its emotional mood.

This writer especially examined the treatment of verses 3-4. Here Jude uses words that are loaded with meaning as to their content and also their *pathos*. In Helm's exegesis of "contend," he makes note of the word's meaning and briefly references the purpose of "enlivening the church of his day to an immediate and intense struggle, a very real fight requiring all of their available energy."[281] Several references to emotional atmosphere may be found throughout Helm's sermonic treatment of Jude.

No contextual tie with the opening and closing paragraphs and the main body of the letter is made. Some comment concerning the warm embrace of Jude's love for his audience that gives a contextual setting to the harsher paragraphs would shed light on Jude's overall emotional tone in the entire letter.

As in previous analyses of Jude's use of "woe" in verse 11, the writer calls attention to the value of understanding Jude's *pathos* in the opening paragraph to provide a helpful setting to interpret the meaning of "woe" in this context. Helm does make reference to Jesus's and John's use of the word. A discussion of the emotional mood in their use of the word would have provided guidance in understanding Jude's.

The writer moves now to Helm's interpretation of Jude's closing section. He does tie verses 20-23 back to the admonition to "contend for the faith"

---

281 Helm, *1 and 2 Peter and Jude*, 295.

in verse 3. Helm rightly points out that Jude's admonition receives helpful direction "with staccato-like urgency just what it means to contend for the faith . . ."[282] Though not making direct reference to the *pathos* involved in these exhortations, he does seem to recognize instinctively the emotional content of Jude's words. This writer indicates that this very often happens in the messages of preachers. The writer further suggests devotional and sermonic works would be more helpful in a complete understanding of Scripture *pathos* as well as *logos*.

Helm again seems to instinctively understand the *pathos* of Jude's repetition of "dear friend" ("beloved"). He says, "We have arrived at the heart of his letter. And the comforting term beloved is again here to greet us."[283]

In these final words of admonition, the writer has indicated previously that there might be some reference to the false teachers when Jude speaks of witnessing that they are to "have mercy . . . with fear, hating even the garment defiled by the flesh" (v. 23). Though Helm does not suggest there might be a reference to witnessing to those Jude has excoriated in his letter's main body, he does touch on the *pathos* of the words when he says, "These verses . . . were written to thrill us . . . To us goes the joy of saving others from the fires of hell."[284]

In the closing doxology found in verses 24-25, Helm discusses briefly the meaning of the words and praise formulas found therein. He does close the chapter and his exegesis of Jude with statements about the importance of believers rendering praise to God. This conclusion would perhaps have been enhanced by dealing with the *pathos* of Jude's words in such a way that his audience could be left standing in their seats, with loud voices shouting, Amen! Again, this writer realizes that though some of the *pathos* of Scripture passages may be interpreted instinctively, devotional and sermonic works could point out this *pathos*.

---

282   Helm, *1 and 2 Peter and Jude*, 325.
283   Ibid., 326.
284   Ibid., 346.

Chapter Seven

Conclusion

At this juncture the writer will bring together the various arguments set forth to demonstrate the correctness of the thesis statement. A restatement of the thesis will be helpful in this regard. Here is the thesis in full:

> Although *pathos* has been recognized as a vital part of discourse since Aristotle included it with his other two modes of persuasion, *ethos* and *logos*, this monograph will argue that *pathos* has not been given adequate consideration in the interpretation of passages of Scripture. This will be demonstrated in the widespread failure of exegetical and devotional works to give a full analysis of Scripture *pathos* in the preparation of a series of text-driven messages from the book of Jude.

Currently in several fields, there seems to be a renewed emphasis on the role of emotions in communicating meaning. In the process of writing this monograph, the writer observes the call for people to tell "their story." This terminology may be seen in a television program called "The Story." The call for people to give their personal experiences as "their story" comes in various areas of life. Those who may have experienced sexual abuse are encouraged to tell "their story." There seems to be the recognition that the communication of feelings adds completeness and fullness to one's experience.

Psychology in terms of counseling individuals through personal problems and struggles gives attention to the part emotion plays in psychological health. As helpful as this may be, those who teach the eternal truths of God's Word cannot abdicate the role emotion plays just to psychology. To do so robs people of the emotional help provided by the Bible and the God who inspired its truths. Elliott says, "When Christian emotions are not present or when harmful emotions are pervasive, it is a warning that the belief system which the New Testament presents has not been grasped and valued. When Christians transfer allegiance from this world to the kingdom of God, their emotions will be transformed."[285] This monograph argues that a lack of adequate interpretation of emotional mood in Scripture deprives people of the opportunity to move in that positive direction for life change in their daily living.

The field of literature should not have exclusive ownership of the area of the emotions either. In his book, *Story*, previously cited in this monograph, McKee builds his whole volume around how writers for movies may put together the elements of narrative into meaningful stories. He understands, however, that stories are important for human existence. He says, "Traditionally human kind has sought the answer (How should a human being lead his life?) to Aristotle's question from the four wisdoms—philosophy, science, religion, art—taking insight from each to bolt together a livable meaning."[286]

In chapter one, the introduction of this monograph, the writer demonstrates that *pathos* has been vital to Old Testament and New Testament discourse in addition to its role in Greek and Roman culture and in Hebrew culture. The writer argues that to fail to take *pathos* interpretation into account in Scripture interpretation leaves such as incomplete and lacking in thorough analysis. The writer's argument in that regard receives proof in chapters three and four which deal with *logos* and *pathos* exegetical interpretation in the book of Jude.

Chapter two, *pathos* and preaching, may be regarded as something of a side note to the main flow of the monograph. However, the chapter argues that the key to *pathos* in preaching without falling into unbiblical manipulation resides in the preacher embodying and transferring to his audience the *pathos* of the given passage from which he is preaching. The chapter also gives some assistance in understanding how areas such as passage genre, vocabulary, and syntax give invaluable assistance to the preacher who desires to

---

285 Elliott, *Faithful Feelings*, 268.
286 McKee, *Story*, 11.

preach the *pathos* of his passage at hand and not his own emotional mood at the time of delivery.

In chapter five, the writer indicates how the faithful preacher may use the insights of *pathos* analysis in the various preaching paragraphs of the book of Jude. This chapter proves the argument of the monograph that *pathos* analysis occupies a prominent role in the proclamation of God's Word. Failure to take such analysis of the emotional tone of Scripture into the preaching moment renders the proclamation of the Word of God less than complete.

This monograph further argues of a widespread lack of attention to *pathos* analysis in exegetical and expository commentaries as well as devotional and sermonic works. Chapter six sustains this argument by a study of selected commentaries and works of the book of Jude. The chapter does indicate that a hopeful trend in linguistic and socio-rhetorical works that give promise of fruitful *pathos* exegesis in the future.

Faithful interpreters of biblical texts must not surrender the whole field of emotions to those who make use of the dynamics of human emotions in the production of movies. The sacred literature of Scripture abounds in stories filled with *pathos* that prove invaluable to the leading of a sound and productive life. This monograph has demonstrated that such interpretation has not been given adequate attention in the book of Jude in particular and in general biblical exegesis.

Gyu suggests five reasons preachers do not use the biblical *pathos* in preaching. "First, it seems that many preachers think that they should follow Paul, who maintained that he did not use rhetoric for evangelizing to the Corinthian Christians in 1 Corinthians 2:1-5. Second, it seems that many preachers think that they can easily, though unintentionally, make the mistake of manipulating listeners through the use of rhetoric. Third, it seems that many preachers equate the use of rhetorical skill (*pathos*) to ignoring the work of the Holy Spirit. Fourth, many preachers interpret the use of rhetorical skill like *pathos* as a neglect of *logos* from the passage. Fifth, preachers do not know how to use the biblical *pathos* in preaching."[287]

The above reasons receive responses in the various chapters of this monograph. First, Paul rejects the improper use of rhetoric in the declaration of the gospel. However, he himself uses any number of rhetorical devices in his

---

287 Kim, "The Right Use of Biblical *Pathos*," 12-16.

letters. Second, an entire chapter discusses the difference between manipulation and motivation. Manipulation does not enter into the interpretation when the *pathos* of the passage itself receives correct exegesis and application. Third, the preacher need not consider the use of *pathos* as a substitute for the power of the Holy Spirit. The same Holy Spirit who inspires the *logos* of Scripture also inspires its *pathos*. Fourth, rather than neglecting passage *logos*, the interpretation of Scripture *pathos* enhances and highlights its content. Further, the *logos* itself conveys *pathos* through word meanings and syntactical structures. Fifth, perhaps most telling, there does seem to be clear evidence that preachers do not know how to use biblical *pathos* in preaching. The suggestions at the conclusion of this chapter will be helpful toward reducing that deficiency.

Perhaps other deeper reasons might also account for the aversion of conservative interpreters of Scripture toward a thorough study of Scripture *pathos*. One might be the conclusion by some that any attention to emotion may invite complications to sensible reason and mental health. The abuse of emotion need not scare conservative exegetes away from a healthy application of biblically sound emotion. Elliott says, "Scholars have gone about the academic discipline of New Testament studies without an informed view of what emotions are and how they operate."[288] This need not be, indeed, must not be if individuals are to be moved away from unhealthy emotions toward healthy, God-honoring emotions.

This writer considers the emphasis of the New Homiletic on feelings to the detriment of content to be a major contributing cause of concern to conservative interpreters. This contributes to an aversion to the study of Scripture *pathos* on the part of conservative exegetes and homileticians. In a perceptive article, David L. Allen shows that the New Homiletic moved the emphasis from propositional truth as found in Scripture to its narratives or stories. He says that, for the New homileticians "the goal of preaching is not the communication of information . . . but rather the evocation of an experience."[289] For the New Homiletic, propositional truth is out and experience, whether in the biblical text, or that of the preacher, or that of the audience becomes primary (Note:

---

288 Elliott, *Faithful Feelings*, 17.

289 David L. Allen, "Preaching and Postmodernism: An Evangelical Comes to the Dance," *The Southern Baptist Journal of Theology SBJT 5/2* (Summer 2001), 64.

Conclusion

See David L. Allen's article, "A Tale of Two Roads: Homiletics and Biblical Authority," *Journal of The Evangelical Theological Society 43.3* (2000): 489-515.) Allen says, "In the past, preaching sought to communicate meaning in a propositional way. Today . . . it is the audience and the preacher together who create the experience of meaning."[290]

While some of the insights of the New Homiletics provide much help in the preaching of the narrative portions of Scripture, the departure from "the existence of truth, the proclamation of truth, and the reception of truth"[291] tends to give conservatives discomfort with addressing the *pathos* of Scripture. Such a low view of Scripture becomes off putting to a conservative. But one may draw from the refreshing wells of biblical *pathos* while at the same time plucking rich truth content from the trees of biblical propositional truth.

This neglect of passage *pathos* results in an incomplete interpretation of its meaning and message. To focus on the message of the text (its *logos*) to the detriment of its emotional content (*pathos*) doesn't do justice to its inspiration. Kuhn says, "Commentators often leave its (Scripture's) effective dimensions unearthed and fail to consider how *pathos* may be employed by the biblical author in the shaping of the narrative."[292] This kind of incomplete interpretation renders Scripture overly intellectual, lacking in reality and having little connection to real life.

Kuhn suggests a reason why biblical scholars spend little time interpreting the emotional appeal of a pericope of Scripture. He says, "Perhaps biblical scholars presume that reflection on the emotional import of biblical texts is the domain of pastors: 'Leave the serious scholarship to the experts, let the preachers exploit whatever emotional appeal they can imaginatively wring from texts for their congregations.'"[293] Preachers will indeed have to do that work, if the scholars continue to neglect this vital area of complete textual understanding. But, far better, the partnership of scholar and pastor holds the promise of a more thorough and complete exegesis of biblical passages.

---

290 David L. Allen, "A Tale of Two Roads: Homiletics and Biblical Authority," *Journal of The Evangelical Theological Society 43.3* (2000): 21-22.

291 Allen, "Preaching and Postmodernism," 68.

292 Kuhn, *The Heart of Biblical Narrative*, 28.

293 Ibid.

THE VITAL ROLE OF *PATHOS* IN A COMPLETE TEXT-DRIVEN INTERPRETATION OF THE BOOK OF JUDE

Kuhn gives three reasons why scholars should give attention to the interpretation of a passage's *pathos*. First, this enables the scholars, and those who read them, to enter into the "literary and rhetorical function" of said passage. Second, pastors tend to follow the pattern set by the scholars' works that they read in the preparation of their sermons. Third, biblical scholars are uniquely trained in the original languages and linguistic and rhetorical disciplines that give them insight into passage *pathos* seldom available to pastors. (Note: Kuhn's discussion in chapter one of his book, *On the Emotions*, provides invaluable help for pastors who need further training in *pathos* interpretation.)

Examining the emotional atmosphere of paragraphs of Scripture broadens one's understanding of Scripture. This examination enables the passage to "speak" in ways not accomplished by mere study of word meanings, syntactical issues, and rhetorical devices that relate only to content. *Pathos* gives tone to how the passage is experienced. For instance, in dialogue are the players angry or happy? Are they inquisitive or assertive? Does their language reflect anger, compassion, disappointment, concern, or conviction? Such attention enables interpreters and proclaimers to give a fuller intellectual and emotional "load" to Scripture. This kind of study should cause those who declare it to rush again to their Bibles and read it with keener eyes. Deep pools of emotion found in Scripture texts will be sources of refreshing waters of understanding.

The importance of *pathos* interpretation can be seen in the preaching paragraphs of Jude as structured in this monograph. The opening (vv. 1-4) and closing (vv. 17-25) paragraphs lovingly envelope the harsher sections in the middle portions (vv. 5-10 and vv. 11-16). To miss this compassionate embrace of its author, Jude, renders the book as something of a rant against the false teachers. The result is an inadequacy of interpretation. *Pathos* interpretation of the envelope avoids this kind of misrepresentation. Jude receives unfair treatment when his love and compassion do not receive proper consideration.

There does seem to be an encouraging trend in the direction of adequate *pathos* interpretation. Several in the field of linguistics are addressing this vital area. Watson's linguistic analyses, as noted in several sections of this monograph, suggest movement in this direction. Ben Witherington's recent works bring to bear upon Scripture interpretation many insights from linguistics and rhetoric.

Conclusion

Further, scholars in the field of preaching are doing ground-breaking work. David L. Allen, a linguistic scholar in his own right, applies linguistic insights to the endeavor of preaching. His emphasis on what he has coined "text-driven preaching" has a variety of areas of study in the volume he edited with Daniel L. Akin and Ned L. Mathews by that name. This writer and Adam Dooley have a chapter dealing specifically with *pathos* interpretation and delivery. (See Chapter 10, "Delivering a Text-Driven Sermon," pp. 243ff).

Barry McCarty's expertise in the field of rhetoric as applied to preaching also constitutes a positive, encouraging development. Further, there is great advantage in the fact that both McCarty and Allen are not only scholars in their field but have the practical experience of serving as pastors for many years. Such a combination uniquely qualifies them to translate their expertise in linguistics and rhetoric to the real world of biblical preaching in a week-by-week congregational setting. A suggestion below will hopefully push work forward in both linguistic and rhetorical studies as they apply to text-driven preaching.

This monograph desires to make a positive contribution to a full-orbed, well-rounded approach to Scripture interpretation. The following are some suggestions to advance the study of Scripture *pathos*:

1. Beginning and continuing this conversation will encourage further scholarly research in the area of *pathos* interpretation. Such study will serve to take the usefulness of biblical scholarship along the road that will pay great dividends to pastors in particular and to the whole of Christendom at large. This writer encourages our brightest young scholars to pursue studies in linguistics and rhetoric as they apply to text-driven preaching. And the writer also strongly suggests that they serve as preaching pastors for a number of years.

2. This monograph suggests that interpreters look again at biblical pericopes through the lens of *pathos* and thereby have a newer, more complete interpretation of Scripture. This exercise will lead to increased spiritual discernment for the church of Jesus Christ. Kuhn summarizes the point quite well: "For when set alongside other interpretive methods aiming to discern how the text was meant to engage its readers, this approach provides yet another opportunity for

biblical scholarship to contribute to the needs of local congregations and helps believers to delve more deeply into the heart of Scripture's witness."[294]

3. Exegetical and sermonic writers are encouraged to give a prominent place to a thorough hermeneutic that includes *pathos* interpretation in all biblical commentaries and works they produce. The writer suggests that a separate section on *pathos* interpretation be included in the commentary and discussion sections of their works on Bible books. A discussion of the importance of *pathos* interpretation along with *logos* interpretation in the introduction would also be vital toward full and complete Scripture interpretation. At this level of sermonic resources, those who write commentaries and other works are encouraged to get the *pathos* studies in a form that can be understood by the preacher at the crossroads and transferable to his preparation and delivery of text-driven sermons. In order to put Scripture *pathos* interpretation on a fast track, the writer further suggests great value could be gained with entire commentaries that highlight *pathos* analysis.

4. Those who teach and preach text-driven messages should make exploration of the emotional mood of the texts an essential part of their preparation and delivery of Scripture. Kuhn says, "a more thoroughgoing engagement with the rhetorical force of the text than is typical of other approaches . . . (puts the interpreter) . . . in the place of Scripture's first readers and (enables us to) imagine what was going on not only in their heads, but also in their hearts . . . it can lead us to discern what fears, hopes, doubts, and joys they experienced . . ."[295] This writer has previously acknowledged that some have an innate awareness of *pathos* in Scripture and are able to communicate it effectively. However, those who are not so gifted will find much benefit in such academic endeavor. And, those who are gifted can find assistance in enhancing their own innate awareness.

---

[294] Kuhn, *The Heart of Biblical Narrative*, 146.
[295] Ibid.

Conclusion

This writer has written and spoken often on the importance of "heart preaching." (See *Power in the Pulpit*, chapter nine, "Making the Connection," pp. 313ff). To grasp how the biblical writer arranges and delivers his message provides invaluable assistance to today's preachers. Kuhn says such assistance "not only better enables them to discern the function of the passage, but also gives them the opportunity to draw from—in ways that are appropriate to their own time and place—the biblical authors' use of *pathos* as a resource for their own faithful proclamation of the text."[296]

The writer has demonstrated the importance of interpreting *pathos* in a Bible book or pericope within that book in such an analysis of the book of Jude. Inadequate exegesis of the loving, compassionate *pathos* of the opening and closing paragraphs of Jude (vv. 1-4, vv. 17-25) may very well cause the exegete and preacher to misinterpret the more severe paragraphs between them (vv. 5-10, vv. 11-16).

The writer received an excellent resource from his major professor, Barry McCarty, to give clarity and clinch the argument of this monograph. In Brooks Landon's volume *Building Great Sentences*, he calls attention to the fact that the mere listing of the various parts of speech, syntactical structure, and dictionary meaning of the words doesn't tell the whole story of a sentence. To illustrate this, he offers an illustration from John Steinbeck. Steinbeck points out "that naming the parts of a fish and cataloging a fish in terms of its structure doesn't actually tell the full story . . . a fish can be rigorously identified by counting its spines . . .,"[297] but that doesn't do justice to the reality of the fish. Then the illustration (paraphrased):

The Mexican sierra has many spines that can be easily counted. However, the fisherman experiences a more complete reality of the fish in actual contact through the fishing experience. The sierra can strike so hard on a line that the fisherman's hands may be burned. Fish sounds, near escapes, finally caught, the sierra comes into the boat with tail beating the air and colors pulsing. This experience with the fish gives a whole new perspective toward the fish than just the counting of the spines in a laboratory. The laboratory experience is

---

[296] Kuhn, *The Heart of Biblical Narrative*, 14.

[297] Brooks Landon, *Building Great Sentences* (New York: A Plume Book, Penguin Group, 2013), 13.

stiff, foul smelling, and provides a lifeless, colorless understanding of the fish. This is a far less reality than the more complete one the fisherman experiences when encountering the fish on a fishing expedition.

Landon adds this telling comment:

> And his point seems to me to apply equally to sentences, and not just because they can also be slippery. Most of the terms we use to identify sentences or to label their parts treat the sentence as something dead, something to be dissected, its parts laid out on a table to be identified. This ignores the fact that what Steinbeck terms a "relational reality" exists between sentences and readers, just as surely and much more frequently with much more usually at stake, than exists between a fisherman and a fish."[298]

He further remarks that sentences should be looked upon as "a thing in motion, an experience, something with which we form a relational reality . . . rather than something stiff and lifeless . . ."[299] For Landon the sentence has "a grammatical phenomenon . . . and a rhetorical phenomenon."[300] Landon says, "Grammar has to do with words, while rhetoric has to do with the way we do things with words. Grammar has to do with words as objects that can be labeled and classified, while rhetoric has to do with the purposes to which we put language, and to the consequences of our efforts."[301]

The same reasoning applies to *pathos* interpretation of Scripture passages as well as *logos* interpretation. Applying Landon's observations concerning sentences to Scripture, this writer would like to add that Scripture not only has a grammatical description that identifies its working parts but also a rhetorical description that identifies the relational reality of the same Scripture.[302]

---

[298] Landon, *Building Great Sentences*, 14.
[299] Ibid.
[300] Ibid.
[301] Ibid.
[302] Ibid., 20. Much of what Landon says about the sentence provides enlightenment in *logos* and *pathos* Scripture interpretation.

Conclusion

The writer concludes this monograph with a similar observation regarding the interpretation of Scripture: There is more to biblical interpretation than the mere lexicon definitions of its words and the syntactical relationships of those words. To end biblical interpretation with an examination of its *logos* alone renders the passage short of the reality that is intended. To paraphrase Steinbecks's wording, such analysis renders the text stiff and colorless. To be sure, Scripture interpretation must always give primacy to the *logos* of a particular passage. However, Scripture *pathos* brings that *logos* to life and enables the reader or hearer to receive the complete message of God's Word that the Holy Spirit intends. To paraphrase Landon's wording, to fail to take into consideration Scripture *pathos* renders the text dissected, its parts laid out and identified in a sermon, but dead and lifeless. Bring text-driven preaching to life with proper interpretation of its *logos* **and** its *pathos*.

Bibliography

REFERENCE WORKS AND GENERAL BOOKS

Achtemeier, Elizabeth. *Creative Preaching: Finding the Words.* Nashville: Abingdon Press, 1980.

Adams, Jay E. *Preaching With a Purpose.* Grand Rapids: Zondervan, 1982.

Akin, Daniel L., David L. Allen, and Ned L. *Mathews. Text-Driven Preaching: God's Word at the Heart of Every Sermon.* Nashville: Broadman and Holman Academic, 2010.

Allen, Ronald J. "Feeling and Form in Biblical Interpretation." *Encounter* 43 (1982).

Allender, D. B. and T. Longman III. *The Cry of the Soul: How Our Emotions Reveal Our Deepest Questions About God.* Colorado Springs: Navpress, 1994.

Alexander, L. C. A. "The Relevance of Greco-Roman Literature and Culture to New Testament Study." In *Hearing the New Testament: Strategies for Interpretation,* ed. J. Green. Grand Rapids: Eerdmans, 1995.

Aristotle. "On Rhetoric." Translated by George A. Kennedy. New York: Oxford University Press, 2007.

_____. *The "Art" of Rhetoric.* Translated by John Henry Freese. LCL. Cambridge, MA: Harvard University Press, 1926.

_____. *The Poetics.* Translated by W. Hamilton Fyfe. LCL. Cambridge: Harvard University Press, 1973.

Arthurs, Jeffrey. *Preaching with Variety: How to Re-create the Dynamics of Biblical Genres.* Grand Rapids, Kregel, 2007.

Averill, J. R. "A Constructivist View of Emotions." In Plutchik and Kellerman (1980).

Bailey, Richard. "Driven by Passion: Jonathan Edwards and the Art of Preaching." In *The Legacy of Jonathan Edwards,* eds. D.G. Hart, Sean Michael Lucas, and Stephen J. Nichols. Grand Rapids: Baker Academic (2003).

Bateman, Herbert W. IV. *Interpreting the General Letters: An Exegetical Handbook.* Series edited by John D. Harvey. Grand Rapids: Kregel, 2013.

Bauer, Walter. *A Greek-Engish Lexicon of the New Testament and Other Early Christian Literature*, 3rd ed. Revised and edited by Frederick William Danker. Translated by William F. Arndt, F. Wilbur Gingrich, and F. W. Danker. Chicago: University of Chicago Press, 2000.

Baxter, J. Sidlow. "Explore the Book." *Acts to Revelation,* vol. 6. London: Marshall, Morgan, and Scott, 1965.

Bickel, R. Bruce, *Light and Heat: The Puritan View of the Pulpit.* Morgan, PA: Soli Deo Gloria Publications, 1999.

Broadus, John A. *A Treatise on the Preparation and Delivery of Sermons,* rev. ed. New York: Richard R. Smith, 1930.

Brooks, Landon. *Building Great Sentences.* New York: A Plume Book, Penguin Group, 2013.

Brown, Gillian and George Yule. *Discourse Analysis.* Cambridge: Cambridge University Press, 1983.

Bullinger, Ernest W. *Figures of Speech Used in the Bible Explained and Illustrated.* Grand Rapids: Baker Book House, 1968.

Burgess, Theodore C. *Epideictic Literature.* Chicago: University of Chicago Studies in Classical Philology 3, 1902.

Chambers, A. "A Biblical Theology of Godly Human Anger." Ph.D. diss., Trinity Evangelical Divinity School, 1996.

Chappell, Bryan. *Christ-Centered Preaching.* Grand Rapids: Baker, 1994.

Charles, J. D. *Literary Strategy in the Epistle of Jude.* London and Toronto: Associated University Presses, 1993.

Childs, R. S. *Introduction to the Old Testament as Scripture.* Philadelphia: Fortress Press, 1979.

Cicero, "De Oratore Books I, II." In *The Loeb Classical Library.* Translated by E. W. Sutton and H. Rackman. Cambridge, MA: Harvard University Press, 1948.

Clark, David J. *Analyzing and Translating New Testament Discourse.* Dallas, Texas: Fontes Press, 2019.

Colson, Charles W. *Kingdom in Conflict.* Grand Rapids: Zondervan Publishing Company, 1987.

Corrigan, John, ed. *Religion and Emotion: Approaches and Interpretation.* Oxford: Oxford University Press, 2004.

Darwin, Charles. *The Expression of the Emotions in Man and Animals.* London: Penguin Books, 2009 (first published in 1872).

DeSousa, R. B. *The Rationality of Emotions.* Cambridge: The MIT Press, 1987.

DiCicco, Mario. *Paul's Use of Ethos, Pathos and Logos in 2 Corinthians 10-13.* Lewison: Mellen Biblical Press Series 31, 1995.

Duduit, Micheal. "Preaching and Passion: An Interview with Robert Smith." *Preaching* 20 (January-February 2005): 18-20.

Edwards, Jonathan. *A Treatise on Religious Affections.* Grand Rapids: Baker Book House, 1982.

_____. "The True Excellency of a Gospel Minister." In *The Works of Jonathan Edwards,* vol. 2. Edinburgh: Banner of Truth, 1974.

Edwards, O. C., Jr. *A History of Preaching.* Nashville: Abingdon, 2004.

Elliott, Matthew A. *Faithful Feelings: Rethinking Emotion in the New Testament.* Grand Rapids: Kregel Academic and Professional, 2006.

Fanning, Buist L. "A Theology of Peter and Jude." In *A Biblical Theology of the New Testament.* Edited by Roy B. Zuck and Darrell L. Bock. Chicago: Moody, 1994.

Ferguson, Sinclair B. "Preaching to the Heart." In *Feed My Sheep: A Passionate Plea for Preaching.* Edited by Don Kistler. Morgan: Soli Deo Gloria Publications, 2002.

Forsythe, P. T. *Positive Preaching and the Modern Mind.* Grand Rapids: Eerdmans, 1964.

Bibliography

Fortenbaugh, W. W. *Aristotle on Emotion*. London: Gerald Duckworth and Company, 1975.

Frank, R. H. *Passions Within Reason: The Strategic Role of Emotions*. New York: Norton, 1988.

Fuller, Charles, *The Trouble with "Truth through Personality": Phillips Brooks, Incarnation and the Evangelical Boundaries of Preaching*. Eugene, OR: Wipf and Stock, 2010.

Greenspan, P. *Emotions and Reasons: An Inquiry Into Emotional Justification*. London: Routledge, 1988.

Harner, Philip B. *What Are They Saying about the Catholic Epistles?* Mahwah: Paulist, 2004.

Hauser, Gerard A. *Introduction to Rhetorical Theory*, 2nd ed. Long Grove, IL: Waveland, 2002.

Hogan, Lucy Lind and Robert Reid. *Connecting with the Congregation: Rhetoric and the Art of Preaching*. Nashville: Abingdon Press, 1999.

Hollifield, Gregory K. "Expository Preaching That Touches the Heart." *Preaching*, http://www.preaching.com/resources/articles/11549461/. Accessed March 7, 2019.

_____. "Expository Preaching That Touches the Heart." *Preaching* 19 (2004).

Hutch, R. A. *Jonathan Edward's Analysis of Religious Experience, JPT*6.

Johnston, Jason. "The Multichiastic Structure of Jude and Its Contribution to the Purpose of the Epistle." Th.M. thesis, Dallas Theological Seminary, 2008.

Lloyd-Jones, Dr. Martyn. *Preachers and Preaching*. Grand Rapids: Zondervan, 2011.

Kennedy, George A. *Classical Rhetoric and Its Christian and Secular Tradition from Ancient to Modern Times,* 2nd ed., rev., and enl. Chapel Hill: The University of North Carolina Press, 1999.

———. *New Testament Interpretation through Rhetorical Criticism.* Chapel Hill: University of North Carolina Press, 1984.

Kennedy, George, trans. and ed. *Aristotle on Rhetoric: A Theory of Civic Discourse.* New York: Oxford University Press, 1991.

Konstan, David. *The Emotions of the Ancient Greeks: Studies in Aristotle and Classical Literature.* Toronto: University of Toronto Press, 2006.

Kuhn, Karl Allen. *The Heart of Biblical Narrative: Rediscovering Biblical Appeal to the Emotions.* Minneapolis: Fortress Press, 2009.

Kuruvilla, Abraham. *Privilege the Text!: A Theological Hermeneutic for Preaching.* Chicago: Moody Publishers, 2003.

Larsen, David L. *The Company of the Preachers: A History of Biblical Preaching from the Old Testament to the Modern Era.* Grand Rapids: Kregel, 1998.

Lazarus, Richard S. and Bernice N. *Passion and Reason: Making Sense of Our Emotions.* Oxford: Oxford University Press, 1994.

Long, Thomas G. *Preaching and the Literary Forms of the Bible.* Minneapolis: Fortress, 1988

Lutzer, E. *Managing Your Emotions.* New York: Christian Herald Books, 1981.

Mack, Burton L. *Rhetoric and the New Testament.* Minneapolis: Fortress Press, 1990.

Martin, R. P. "The Theology of Jude, I Peter and 2 Peter." In *The Theology of the Letters of James, Peter and Jude, New Testament Theology.* Cambridge: Cambridge University Press, 1994.

McCall, Marsh. "Ancient Rhetorical Theories of Simile and Comparison." *Loeb Classical Monographs.* Cambridge: Harvard University Press, 1969.

McKee, Robert. *Story: Substance, Structure, Style, and the Principles of Screenwriting.* New York: Harper Collins Publishers, 1997.

Mehrabian, Albert. *Non-verbal Communication.* New York: Routledge, 2017.

Morgan, G. Campbell. *Living Messages of the Books of the Bible,* vol. 2. New York: Fleming H. Revell, 1912.

Nussbaum, Martha C. *Upheavals of Thought: The Intelligence of Emotions.* Cambridge: Cambridge University Press, 2001.

Olford, Stephen F. *Anointed Expository Preaching.* Nashville: B & H Publishing, 1998.

Osburn, C. D. "Discourse Analysis and Jewish Apocalyptic in the Epistle of Jude." In *Linguistics and New Testament Interpretation: Essays on Discourse Analysis.* Nashville: Broadman (1992): 287-319.

Owen, John. *The Works of John Owen*, 3rd ed., vol. 6. Edited by William H. Goold. Carlisle, PA: Banner of Truth, 1977.

Piper, John, Brothers. *We Are Not Professionals: A Plea to Pastors for Radical Ministry.* Nashville, TN: Broadman & Holman, 2012.

Prideaux, John. *Sacred Eloquence: The Art of Rhetoric as It Is Laid Down in Scripture.* London: George Sawbridge, 1956.

Quintillian. *The Orator's Education.* Translated by Donald A. Russell. Cambridge, MA: Harvard University Press, 2001.

Robbins, Vernon K. *Exploring the Texture of Texts: A Guide to Socio-Rhetorical Interpretation.* Valley Forge: Trinity Press International, 1996.

Robertson, A. T. "Word Pictures in the New Testament." In *General Epistles and Revelation of John,* vol. 6. Nashville: Broadman, 1933.

Robinson, Haddon W. *Biblical Preaching.* Grand Rapids: Baker, 2001.

Shaddix, Jim. *The Passion-Driven Sermon.* Nashville: Broadman and Holman, 2003.

Sherman, R. C. *The Passions.* Notre Dame: Notre Dame University Press, 1976.

Smith, Steven W. *Recapturing the Voice of God: Shaping Sermons Like Scripture.* Nashville: Broadman and Holman Academic, 2015.

Solomon, R. C. *The Passions.* New York: Doubleday, 1976.

Spencer, F. Scott, ed. *Mixed Feelings and Vexed Passions.* Atlanta: SBL Press, 2017.

Spurgeon, Charles. *Lectures to My Students.* London: Marshal, Morgan, and Scott, 1954.

Stout, Harry S. *The Divine Dramatist: George Whitefield and the Rise of Modern Evangelicalism.* Grand Rapids: Eerdmans, 1991.

Talbot, Mark S. "Godly Emotions (Religious Affections)." In *A God Entranced Vision of All Things.* Edited by John Piper and Justin Taylor. Wheaton: Crossway Books, 2004.

Vines, Jerry and Jim Shaddix. *Power in the Pulpit: How to Prepare and Deliver Expository Sermons,* rev. ed. Chicago: Moody Publishers, 1999, 2017.

_____. *Progress in the Pulpit: How to Grow in your Preaching.* Chicago: Moody Publishers, 2017.

Vines, Jerry and Adam Dooley. *Passion in the Pulpit: How to Exegete the Emotion of Scripture.* Chicago: Moody Publishers, 2018.

Walton, Brad. *Jonathan Edwards, Religious Affections and the Puritan Analysis of True Piety, Spiritual Sensation and Heart Religion.* Lewiston: The Edwin Mellen Press, 2002.

Watson, Duane Frederick. *Invention, Arrangement, and Style: Rhetorical Criticism of Jude and II Peter.* Atlanta: Scholars Press, 1988.

Webb, R. L. "The Eschatology of the Epistle of Jude and Its Rhetorical and Social Functions." *Bulletin for Biblical Research* 6 (1996).

_____. "The Use of 'Story' in the Letter of Jude: Rhetorical Strategies of Jude's Narrative Episodes." *Journal for the Study of the New Testament* 31 (2008).

Webb, R. L. and P. H. Davids, ed. "Reading Jude with New Eyes: Methodological Reassessments of the Letter of Jude." *Library of New Testament Studies.* London: T and T Clark, 2008.

Wendland, R. R. "A Comparative Study of 'Rhetorical Criticism,' Ancient and Modern, with Special Reference to the Larger Structure and Function of the Epistle of Jude." *Neotestamentica* 28 (1994).

Wiersbe, Warren. *Preaching and Teaching with Imagination.* Wheaton: Victor Books/SP Publications, 1994.

_____. *Walking With Giants.* Grand Rapids: Baker, 1976

Witherington, Ben III. *Letters and Homilies for Jewish Christians: A Socio-Rhetorical Commentary on Hebrews, James and Jude.* Downers Grove: InterVarsity Press, 2007.

Wolthuis, T. R. "Jude and the Rhetorician: A Dialogue on the Rhetorical Nature of the Epistle of Jude." *CTJ* 24 (1989).

Wuest, Kenneth. *In These Last Days: II Peter, I, II, III John, and Jude in the New Testament.* Grand Rapids: Eerdmans, 1954.

York, Hershael W. and Bert Decker. *Preaching With Bold Assurance.* Nashville: Broadman and Holman, 2003.

Zajonc, R. B. "Feeling and Thinking. Preferences Need No Interferences." *American Psychologist* (1980) 35:151-74.

Exegetical and Devotional Commentaries on Jude

Allison, B. Gray. *Now Unto Him: Messages from Jude for Our Day.* Jackson: C and S Printing Co., Inc., 1964.

Arichea, Daniel C. and Howard A. Hatton. "A Handbook on the Letter from Jude and the Second Letter from Peter." *UBS Handbook Series.* New York: United Bible Societies, 1993.

Barclay, William. "The Letters of John and Jude." *The Daily Study Bible Series*, 2nd ed. Philadelphia: The Westminster Press, May 1960.

Barnett, A. E. and E. G. Homrighausen. "The Second Episle of Peter and the Epistle of Jude." In the *Interpreter's Bible*, vol. 12. New York: Abingdon, 1957.

Bateman, Herbert W., IV. "Jude." *Evangelical Exegetical Commentary.* Bellingham: Lexham Press, 2018.

Bauckham, Richard J. "Jude, 2 Peter." *Word Biblical Commentary*, vol. 50. Waco: Word Books, Publisher, 1983.

Bibliography

_____. *Word Biblical Themes: Jude, II Peter.* Waco: Word Books, 1990.

Bigg, Charles. "Epistles of Jude, 2 Peter." *WBC* 50. Waco: Word Books, 1983.

Blum, Edwin. "Jude." *The Expositor's Bible Commentary*, vol. 12. Edited by Frank Gaebelein. Grand Rapids: Zondervan, 1981.

Brosend II, William F. *James and Jude.* Cambridge: Cambridge University Press, 2004.

Calvin, John. "A Harmony of the Gospels Matthew, Mark, and Luke. James and Jude." *Calvin's New Testament Commentaries.* Translated by A. W. Morrison. Grand Rapids: Eerdmans, 1975.

Cedar, Paul A. "James, 1, 2 Peter, Jude." *Comunicator's Commentary Series.* Waco: Word, 1984.

Christian Standard Bible, "The Holy Bible." Nashville: Holman Bible Publishers, 2017.

Craddock, Fred B. "First and Second Peter and Jude." *Westminster Bible Companion.* Louisville: Westminster John Knox, 1995.

Cranfield, C. E. B. "I and 2 Peter and Jude." *Torch Bible Commentaries.* London: SCM Press, 1960.

Davids, Peter H. *2 Peter and Jude: A Handbook on the Greek Text.* Waco: Baylor University Press, 2011.

Dennison, James T., Jr. "The Structure of the Epistle of Jude." *Kerus* 29/1-May 2014.

Green, M. "The Second Epistle of Peter and the Epistle of Jude." In *TNTC*. Grand Rapids: Eerdmans, 1968.

THE VITAL ROLE OF *PATHOS*
IN A COMPLETE TEXT-DRIVEN INTERPRETATION OF THE BOOK OF JUDE

Greenlee, J. Harold. *An Exegetical Summary of Jude*. Dallas: Summer Institute of Linguistics, 1999.

Hawkins, O. S. *In Sheep's Clothing: Jude's Urgent Warning about Apostasy in the Church*. Neptune: Loizeaux, 1994.

Helm, David R. *1 and 2 Peter and Jude*. Wheaton: Crossway, 2008.

Hillyer, N. "1 and 2 Peter, Jude." In *NIBC*. Peabody: Hendrickson Publishers, 1992.

Ironside, H. A. *Exposition of the Epistle of Jude*, rev. ed. New York: Loizeaux Brothers, 1900.

Kelly, J. N. D. "The Epistles of Peter and Jude." *BNTC*. Grand Rapids: Baker Book House, 1981.

Lucas, Dick and Christopher Green. *The Message of 2 Peter and Jude*. Downers Grove: InterVarsity Press, 1995.

MacArthur, John. *Beware The Pretenders*. Fullerton: Victor Books, 1980.

Maclaren, Alexander. "Exposition of Holy Scripture." *Epistles of Peter, Epistles of John, Jude, Revelation, General Index*, vol. 11. Grand Rapids: Eerdman, 1959.

Mayor, Joseph B. *The Epistle of St. Jude and the Second Epistle of St. Peter*. Grand Rapids: Baker Book House, 1979.

Neyrey, Jerome. "2 Peter, Jude." *Anchor Bible*, vol. 37C. New York: Doubleday, 1993.

Perkins, Pheme. "First and Second Peter, James, and Jude." *Interpretation: A Bible Commentary for Teaching and Preaching*. Louisville: John Knox Press, 1995.

Phillips, John. *Exploring the Epistle of Jude*. Grand Rapids: Kregel, 2001.

Schreiner, Thomas R. "1, 2 Peter, Jude." *The New American Commentary*, vol. 37. Nashville: Broadman and Holman Publishers, 2003.

Sidebottom, E. M. "James, Jude, 2 Peter." *The New Century Bible Commentary*. Grand Rapids: Eerdmans, 1967.

Wiersbe, Warren. *Be Alert*. Wheaton: Victor, 1984.

Dissertations, Articles, and Unpublished Works

Allen, David L., "A Tale of Two Roads: Homiletics and Biblical Authority." *Journal of The Evangelical Theological Society* 43.3(2000): 489-515.

_____, "Preaching and Postmodernism: An Evangelical Comes to the Dance." *The Southern Baptist Journal of Theology SBJT* 5/2 (Summer 2001).

Dennison, James T., Jr. "The Structure of the Epistle of Jude." *Kerux: The Journal of Northwest Theological Seminary* 29/1 (May, 2014).

Dooley, Adam. "Utilizing Biblical Persuasion Techniques in Preaching Without Being Manipulative." Ph.D. Diss. presented to the faculty of The Southern Baptist Theological Seminary, May 2006.

Edwards, Jeffrey L. "The Literary Structure of Jude and How It Affects the Interpretation of 'the Faith' in Jude 3." Research Paper, Baptist Bible Seminary, Clarks Summit, April 2012.

Edwards, Jonathan. "The True Excellency of a Gospel Minister." In *The Works of Jonathan Edwards*, vol.2. Edinburgh: Banner of Truth, 1974.

Gilmore, John. *Sick Crank or Sound Critic?: Jude's Role and Relevance in the Church—Then and Now*. Unpublished Work, May, 1998.

Heisler, Gregory. "A Case for a Spirit-Driven Methodology of Expository Preaching." Ph.D. Diss., The Southern Baptist Theological Seminary, 2003.

Hirsch, E. D. "Transhistorical Intentions and the Persistence of Allegory." *New Literary History* 25(1994): 549-67.

Hollifield, Greggory K. "Expository Preaching That Touches the Heart." *Preaching* 19 (2004): 18-23.

_____. "Expository Preaching That Touches the Heart." *Preaching* 19, No. 5 (2010): 18.

Howell, Mark A., "Hermeneutical Bridges and Homiletical Methods: A Comparative Analysis of the New Homiletic and Expository Preaching Theory 1970-1995." A dissertation presented to the faculty of Southeastern Baptist Theological Seminary, Wake Forest, North Carolina, 1999.

Kim, Sung Gyu. "The Right Use of Biblical *Pathos* in Persuasive Preaching." Diss., Biola University, ProQuest Dissertations Publishing, 2013.3563286.

Perkins, Pheme. "First and Second Peter, James, and Jude." *Interpretation: A Bible Commentary for Teaching and Preaching*. Louisville: John Knox Press, 1995.

Rowston, Douglas J. "The Setting of the Letter of Jude." Ph.D. Diss., Southern Baptist Theological Seminary, 1971.

Vines, Jerry. "Preaching Through Jude." *The Southwestern Journal of Theology*. Paige Patterson, Editor-in-Chief, vol. 58 no. 1. Fall, 2015.

Wells, David. "The Theology of Preaching: The Biblical World in the Contemporary World." *Journal of The Evangelical Homiletics Society* 9, no. 1 (March 2009): 24.

York, Hershael W. "An Analysis and Synthesis of the Exegetical Methods of Rhetorical Criticism and Discourse Analysis as Applied to the Structure of First John." Dissertation, Mid-America Baptist Theological Seminary, 1993.

Appendix

Literature Review and Works Cited

Akin, Daniel L., David L. Allen, and Ned L. Mathews. *Text-Driven Preaching: God's Word at the Heart of Every Sermon*. Nashville: Broadman and Holman Academic, 2010, 315 pages.

    In some ways this series of essays about text-driven preaching is the seminal volume that introduces contemporary exegetes, teachers, and preachers to the importance of dealing with what a biblical passage actually says. Several chapters in the work touch on the vital role of Scripture *pathos* in an adequate and complete exegesis of the text. The book also contains essays that will assist those who preach and teach the Word of God in not only considering *pathos* as a hermeneutical tool in the interpretation of Scripture passages, but as a homiletical tool in the composition of text-driven messages as well.

Bateman, Herbert W., IV. "Jude." *Evangelical Exegetical Commentary.* Bellingham: Lexham Press, 2015, 486 pages.

    Bateman will be used as an example of the need for more attention to *pathos* in the majority of exegetical works available to those who would thoroughly analyze biblical passages.

Bauckham, Richard J. "Jude, 2 Peter." *Word Biblical Commentary*, Volume 50. Waco: Word Books, Publisher, 1983, 357 pages.

Bauckham's commentary gives further evidence of the need for exegetical and expository commentaries to give more attention to the *pathos* content in Jude and by extension, to other commentaries on Scripture.

Dooley, Adam. "Utilizing Biblical Persuasion Techniques in Preaching Without Being Manipulative." Ph.D. dissertation presented to the faculty of The Southern Baptist Theological Seminary, May 2006, 167 pages.

Dooley's Ph.D. dissertation will be an important source for a complete understanding of the necessity of interpreting passage *pathos* as it relates to sermon persuasion that is biblically sound and not manipulative.

Elliott, Matthew A. *Faithful Feelings: Rethinking Emotion in the New Testament.* Grand Rapids: Kregel Academic and Professional, 2006, 301 pages.

Elliott's work will be an important contribution to the role of *pathos* in New Testament passages. In particular, its role in a thorough exegesis of the book of Jude gives helpful direction.

Gilmore, John. *Sick Crank or Sound Critic?: Jude's Role and Relevance in the Church—Then and Now.* Unpublished work, May, 1998.

Though Gilmore's work on the book of Jude is unpublished, it is very helpful in understanding the necessity and helpfulness of a correct understanding of biblical *pathos* in Jude. His insights are unique and intriguing. They provide a helpful framework for the examination of *pathos* in all areas of biblical interpretation. This monograph will draw upon this work to illustrate the vital role of *pathos* interpretation in Jude, and by extension, in all Scripture interpretation.

Heisler, Gregory. "A Case for a Spirit-Driven Methodology of Expository Preaching." Ph.D. dissertation, The Southern Baptist Theological Seminary, 2003.

Heisler's dissertation throws light upon the Holy Spirit's role in the use of *pathos* analysis in Scripture. Because the Holy Spirit is the divine author of Scripture, its *pathos* as well as its *logos* is Spirit-inspired. This being the case, no exegesis of biblical passages is complete until its *pathos* is also exegeted. Heisler is the only scholar this writer has read thus far who acknowledges the role of the Holy Spirit in a complete examination of Scripture passages.

Helm, David R. *1 and 2 Peter and Jude.* Wheaton: Crossway, 2008.

Helm is one of the newer works on the book of Jude. Sermonic in nature, there is some attention to its *pathos*, but very little. This volume will be used as another example of the need for devotional and sermonic works to give more attention to passage *pathos*.

Kennedy, George A. *Classical Rhetoric and Its Christian and Secular Tradition from Ancient to Modern Times,* second edition, revised and enlarged. Chapel Hill: The University of North Carolina Press, 1999.

This classic work by Kennedy will be constantly referenced in the earlier chapters of the monograph. His recognized scholarship in the historical aspects of classical rhetoric is vital to the earlier chapters of the monograph in providing a framework to understand the importance of *pathos* as it applies to Scripture. The anticipation is that this work will be cited often and extensively.

Kim, Sung Gyu. "The Right Use of Biblical *Pathos* in Persuasive Preaching." Dissertation, Biola University, ProQuest Dissertations Publishing, 2013.3563286.

Kim's dissertation is the closest one found that specifically discusses the theme of this monograph. Though unnecessarily lengthy, there are many areas that are very informative and useful in moving forward the argument set forth in the anticipated thesis argument of this monograph.

Konstan, David. *The Emotions of the Ancient Greeks: Studies in Aristotle and Classical Literature.* Toronto: University of Toronto Press, 2006, 422 pages.

    Konstan's work is a helpful source alongside Kennedy's historical survey of the role of the emotions in Greek culture. Konstan provides additional insights that are helpful in this monograph.

Kuhn, Karl Allen. *The Heart of Biblical Narrative: Rediscovering Biblical Appeal to the Emotions.* Minneapolis: Fortress Press, 2009, 181 pages.

    Kuhn addresses the role of the emotions in the narrative portions of the Bible. Though not specifically applicable to the book of Jude, the insights Kuhn brings to the monograph subject provide a helpful understanding that biblical passages, whether narrative or otherwise, cannot be adequately understood and preached unless the emotional tone of those passages is ascertained and communicated.

Kuruvilla, Abraham. *Privilege the Text!: A Theological Hermeneutic for Preaching.* Chicago: Moody Publishers, 2003.

    Kuruvilla helpfully takes Ricouer's concepts of the worlds before, in, and beyond the text and applies them to the preaching of the Word of God. Though not easy to understand, the fruits of his insights are well worth the time spent in studying and comprehending what he shares.

Nussbaum, Martha C. *Upheavals of Thought: The Intelligence of Emotions.* Cambridge: Cambridge University Press, 2001, 751 pages.

    Nussbaum is considered today's authority on the subject of the emotions. The essays in her volume give some general understanding of what emotion is and how human emotions constitute a vital component to life in its fullest.

Phillips, John. *Exploring the Epistle of Jude.* Grand Rapids: Kregel, 2001.

    The writer will give clear reference to the helpfulness of Phillips' works. Though not trained in formal rhetoric or linguistics, Phillips provides excellent sermonic help in the preparation of Bible messages. Further, the writer listened to Phillips on numerous occasions. Like writer, Phillips's preaching seems to instinctively grasp and communicate passage *pathos*.

Robbins, Vernon K. *Exploring the Texture of Texts: A Guide to Socio-Rhetorical Interpretation.* Valley Forge: Trinity Press International, 1996, 148 pages.

    Robbins demonstrates that texts have layers. Among those layers Robbins shows how emotional mode is an essential part of the texture of Scripture passages. Failure to understand this and to thoroughly examine that layer leads to an inadequate interpretation of Scripture.

Shaddix, Jim. *The Passion-Driven Sermon.* Nashville: Broadman and Holman, 2003.

    Shaddix's work is a helpful contribution to an understanding of the role of *pathos* in text-driven preaching. This work will be helpful in the section of the monograph that explains the role of passage *pathos* in the preaching event.

Spencer, F. Scott, editor. *Mixed Feelings and Vexed Passions.* Atlanta: SBL Press, 2017, 394 pages.

    This book of essays has several discussions that will add helpful information to the monograph. "The Central Role of Emotions in Biblical Theology . . ." and "Getting a Feel for the 'Mixed' and 'Vexed' Study of Emotions in Biblical Literature" will be referenced in the monograph.

Vines, Jerry and Jim Shaddix. *Power in the Pulpit: How to Prepare and Deliver Expository Sermons,* revised edition. Chicago: Moody Publishers, 1999, 2017, 438 pages.

    Vines and Shaddix make some introductory ventures into the subject of *pathos* in the preparation and delivery of expository sermons. There will be some reference to those references.

THE VITAL ROLE OF *PATHOS* IN A COMPLETE TEXT-DRIVEN INTERPRETATION OF THE BOOK OF JUDE

Vines, Jerry and Jim Shaddix. *Progress in the Pulpit: How to Grow in your Preaching.* Chicago: Moody Publishers, 2017, 237 pages.

    This volume will be helpful in that it shows the progress being made in the use of rhetorical devices in current preaching instruction and delivery.

Vines, Jerry and Adam Dooley. *Passion in the Pulpit: How to Exegete the Emotion of Scripture.* Chicago: Moody Publishers, 2018, 206 pages.

    This book in particular gives a rather complete examination of the importance of ascertaining the emotional mode in a biblical passage. Several sections of the monograph will draw heavily upon this work.

Watson, Duane Frederick. *Invention, Arrangement, and Style: Rhetorical Criticism of Jude and II Peter.* Atlanta: Scholars Press, 1988.

    Watson's linguistic volume demonstrates that linguists are on the cutting edge of *pathos* study. This volume especially illustrates this in the references to the *pathos* to be found in the book of Jude.

Witherington, Ben, III. *Letters and Homilies for Jewish Christians: A Socio-Rhetorical Commentary on Hebrews, James and Jude.* Downers Grove: InterVarsity Press, 2007, 656 pages.

    Witherington is a current exegete who understands and utilizes the importance of *pathos* interpretation of Scripture. This particular volume will enable the writer to move the monograph closer to the book of Jude and its various emotional expressions.

www.ingramcontent.com/pod-product-compliance
Lightning Source LLC
Chambersburg PA
CBHW050251010526
44107CB00003B/280